Professional Pascal

23. 11. 99. 2

70 — 11 — 14 — 2

Gurdwara Sri Guru Singh Sabha, Southall

SGSS

Southall

Item no.   007039

43 – D

Henry Ledgard

Professional Pascal

Essays on the Practice of Programming

▲▼▼
Addison-Wesley Publishing Company

Reading, Massachusetts • Menlo Park, California • Don Mills, Ontario
Wokingham, England • Amsterdam • Sydney • Singapore • Tokyo
Madrid • Bogotá • Santiago • San Juan

Library of Congress Cataloging-in-Publication Data

Ledgard, Henry F., 1943—
    Professional pascal.

    Bibliography: p.
    1. Pascal (Computer program language) I. Title.
QA76.73.P2L425 1986   005.13'3   85-30788
ISBN 0-201-11776-2

Photographer: Howard Karger, Montague, Massachusetts

Copyright © 1986 by Henry Ledgard. All rights reserved. No part of this publication may be reproduced, stored in a retrieval system, or transmitted, in any form by any means, electronic, mechanical, photocopying, recording, or otherwise, without the prior written permission of the publisher. Printed in the United States of America. Published simultaneously in Canada.

ABCDEFGHIJ-HA-89876

Contents

Part II: The Culture of Pascal

Part III: Putting It Together

In the past twenty years, the proliferation of research, courses, and seminars in the field of computer science (in its broadest possible conception) has been proportional to the population increase of Silicon Valley. The lead paragraph of a front-page *New York Times* article describes the situation:

> Computer science, a field in which there was no major at most colleges and universities before 1970, is fast becoming one of the most popular majors as enrollments grow so rapidly that some schools must limit admissions. (*The New York Times,* January 14, 1985, p. 1)

This phenomenon may be a mixed blessing. When these efforts are properly structured, as two or three that I shall describe momentarily, new ideas are propounded, old ones are crystallized, and meaningful benefits accrue. But I often wonder: when is real intelligence exchanged—for instance, between teacher and student, or between lecturer and participant in seminars.

Origins of This Work

In 1970, I happened into a conversation with members of the staff at Johns Hopkins University. The conversation had something to do with what we were teaching students. One of the group said something to the effect that we had a great deal to learn about programming. In his course, he was teaching something about restricting the use of control structures and programming in a rather top-down fashion. Most of us had been programming for years, and I didn't see why all of this was particularly important. But later, when I began thinking about it, my own and several other programming projects with which I was involved were hardly successful. Maybe he was on to something.

The person turned out to be Harlan Mills, now recognized as one of the early leaders in today's modern approach to programming. And he was right on target. There was a problem in programming fifteen years ago and there is one today—a giant problem.

During the next few years, I embarked on several projects centering on the study of programming. Some were research projects that concentrated on measuring program complexity. I soon found myself in a thicket of thorns. In an attempt to define the parameters, both technical and human, that focus on measuring program complexity. I have come to believe that only broad approaches to human comprehension can succeed. More importantly, my efforts in this research set the tone for what has become a serious interest in my professional life—the quality of programming as evidenced in its product. In short, the *quality* of software.

With the help of others, I set off on a project writing a sequence of books that are generally known as *The Programming Proverbs*. These books are basically a series of short, amusing essays on various topics in programming. For example, some of the proverbial sayings were: "Think first, code later"; "Make constants constant"; and "Don't leave the reader in the dust." Looking back on these little books, I believed they were on the right track, although the books only scratched the surface.

In 1977 I had the opportunity to participate in the Ada® project, the design of a new programming language. (Ada is a registered trademark of the U.S. government, Ada Joint Program Office.) At once, many issues arose about the design of programs. During this project, taste and craftsmanship were visible design issues. Just like the informal conversations in academia, spirited interchanges turned on such issues as the role of program modules, the potential of separate compilation, and even the nature and politics, if you will, of a team effort. Seemingly innocuous issues were given new meaning, such as the appropriate use or nonuse of comments or the implications of program layout.

In 1983 I had the opportunity to participate in several seminars offered as a "Senior Software Engineering Course" from Philips Electronics. The design of this course is outstanding. The "students" are professional software engineers, with both limited and extensive experience in the field. For seven weeks the participants close themselves from their normal working environment and devote their full efforts to the course. This is a credit to their management, for many organizations see little need for significant postacademic training.

My own experience in this course as tutor has, I hope, been the same for the participants. At some stage, every idea that I thought to be important about programming was raised, challenged, or amplified. It seemed to me that I was, once again, among a circle of friends discussing the same question: What are we doing? But this time with professional programmers and software engineers. Ideas and understanding were changing hands and all of us were gaining a sharpened understanding of the quality of software.

What is Professional Practice

Some would argue that software quality is mainly a matter of design, that is, the choice of appropriate algorithms, data structures, and overall program organization. This view holds that the quality of software is mainly a technical matter, that issues such as craftsmanship, program style, and programming teams are of secondary importance. Opposing this approach, I ask: If one has a beautiful algorithm or data structure, why not show it in the clearest possible manner? How do we write programs so that intent is clear in written form? The journals are filled with papers that identify software's problem to be one of maintenance.

For me it has come down to this: What can we do to prevent the heaps of (basically) rubbish that are presented to management, marketed, and endorsed as professional software?

For example, issues like commenting, program layout, and naming seem like modest, even humble, tasks. But in practice, I submit, such humble issues have a great impact. In a project, these issues arise over and over again, every day. Their frequency is so great that in some cases they can swamp out almost everything else. Good ideas can be buried in impenetrable code. The unwitting programmer, who is not aware of the scope and subtlety of these issues, may not even realize that he or she is trying to work in a self-created swamp of complexity. And when the product of this effort is passed on, others, too, are dragged into the quagmire.

Organization of This Work

This work, then, is my best statement about a number of issues in the *practice* of programming. The book is organized around a series of essays. Each essay relates, directly or indirectly, to the quality of programs. It does not cover all the issues. Some topics are beyond the scope of this work. These include software engineering, management techniques, resource estimating, high-level design notations, and the software lifecycle.

This work is derived, in part, from a larger work on professional programming practice in general. This Pascal version is organized into three sections. The first section deals exclusively with programs themselves. It treats such topics as the role of program comments, the persistence of global variables, and the use of types. The underlying theme of these essays is to build a sense of careful craftsmanship in programming. This section concludes with the observation that it is not unreasonable to expect programs to work the first time they are run—a view that may seem to be a flight of fancy for some readers.

The second section treats a few issues that are mainly relevant to the Pascal culture, for instance, the subtleties in Standard Pascal.

The final section presents an annotated example. In developing this example, a good number of ideas mentioned in previous essays are put to practice. The section concludes with a substantive program, with annotations.

Acknowledgments

A number of people have personally influenced this work, either through my thinking about the issues or by motivating my desire to take on this effort. These include Harlan Mills, William Cave, Dan McCracken, Jean Ichbiah, and David

Gries. Over many years, Andrew Singer offered me a stimulating critique of the areas of programming and human engineering. Jon Hueras has, for me, been a model of the true professional software engineer. Michael Marcotty offered insights into many issues addressed here. Richard Rasala (Northeastern University) provided an extensive and penetrating review. Jerry Waxman (Queens College, New York), Richard Rinewalt (University of Texas at Arlington), and Charles Engelke (University of Florida in Gainesville) provided helpful review comments.

In addition to taking most of the photographs that appear in this work, Howard Karger helped design how the chapter concepts were interpreted photographically.

The Philips courses, where I gained a greater understanding of software quality, were under the brilliant and inspired direction of Allen Macro, assisted by John Buxton. Nat Macon, my colleague, as well as the participants in these courses, strengthened my commitment to excellence and teaching.

John Tauer, a professional from another discipline, assisted me on this work with his gifted pen and mind. He turned a table at Daisy's into a forum for discussing the very heart of professional practice.

H. L.

This book contains many programming examples. A good percentage represent poor programming practice. The examples are my own, but they are not idle invention. Although they are invented, they represent the "state of the art" of practitioners, as I have witnessed many, many times over.

This book is also my considered opinion about professional practice. The thoughtful reader may, in places, have good reason to hold other views. This should not confuse our common pursuit for excellence.

Typeface Note:

This book has been typeset using a monospaced font (both bold and nonbold) for programs. Monospaced typefaces, with or without bold, are most appropriate for programs. They promote readability and, I believe, give the best appearance for printing programs.

Something is Wrong, Hear

When a friend of mine was nearing the end of his graduate studies, a kindly mentor gave him advice roughly along these lines: "No matter what you do in the future, whether you choose to be a programmer, a writer, a teacher, take time— nay, *make* time—for reflection." The subsequent essays are, I suppose, a product of many hours of reflection, wondering about the practical issues that programmers face each day and the way they deal with them.

Programming requires that we translate the language that we speak every day into a language that works for a computer. In so doing, we are describing reality in a different, abstract way to solve problems. But there is a craftsmanship in programming that is often more difficult to grasp than the abstraction. It seems to me that terms such as clarity, simplicity, balance, symmetry, and precision are useful synonyms for an overworked adjective: "beautiful."

These "beauties" come to mind in Lincoln's Gettysburg Address. Suppose, for some reason, he had written:

> Eighty-seven years ago, our antecedents created a novel nation-state in this hemisphere, the principles being that the citizenry should live in freedom, and that every citizen would be equal in every manner to one another.

Says the same thing, doesn't it? But something's wrong. Somehow the simplicity and elegance are missing. And yet, today, no sportswriter would dare to submit copy to his editor saying that the course record at Such-and-Such Golf Club was broken when an unknown amateur shot "three score and three." There are words for the times and times for the words.

The substance of this discussion is that in many moments of reflection on this issue or that abstraction, on this line of code or that program, I have come to feel that "something is wrong here." A few cases are easy to spot:

- An expression that carries on for four or five lines.
- Two lengthy procedures that are identical except for a line or two.
- A subroutine that is five times longer than it should be.
- An expression that is illogical to read.

Others, in fact most, are more difficult to see.

So, before we begin the subsequent essays on programming practice, some examples are offered. The purpose of these examples is threefold:

1. To sketch the territory of issues treated in this work.
2. To raise certain questions about programming practice.
3. To sharpen awareness of program quality.

On each example, you might ask: Why does a programmer take a particular route in the first place? What was the underlying logic? And why, when someone *else* looks at the work, do problems of reading, interpretation, and understanding arise?

Some of the examples that follow are short, innocuous statements—others are longer and· require some insight. That is, if you take some time for "reflection" about what is being attempted in each example, you will be asking yourself: "What is wrong here?" You may answer by posing other questions.

. . . .

Example 1

```
procedure UPDATETABLE;
{ This procedure prints... }
```

Example 2

```
procedure CHECKLINE(LINE:STRING; LINELENGTH: INTEGER;
                    STR: STRING; STRLENGTH: INTEGER; var
                    FOUND: BOOLEAN; var STARTPOS: INTEGER);
```

Example 3

```
SETLINE (12);
WRITE ('Enter next amount:');
READLN (INVAL)
```

. . . .

For these first three examples, let me raise questions that I have asked. Let us examine Example 1.

- Is the procedure misnamed?
- Does it update a table?
- Does it do other things, including printing?
- Is it a procedure that has one purpose or multiple purposes?

If you can't give a procedure a simple and clear name, there is something wrong with its formulation, that is, it is not a one-purpose procedure. Look at the example one more time. In name we are *updating,* but we are in fact *printing!* Something's wrong here.

Example 2 requires a little more mental concentration.

- Which parameters are inputs?
- Which are outputs?
- Is there a punctuation error?
- For the *reader,* what does it *look* like? Is it messy, or does it have balance and symmetry?

Well, there is some logic here. The first four parameters are inputs, and the last two are outputs. But why does the reader have to look for them? The programmer gave little thought to how the reader could identify the parameters without undue effort.

Example 3 presents a prompting message given to the user on line 12, and the value is supplied immediately after the prompt (with no intervening space).

- What is special about line 12?
- Will the user be uncomfortable to see "amount:51"?
  (*Hint:* Why not "amount: 51"?)
- Is INVAL a good name?
  (*Hint:* Why not INPUTVALUE? Or better, call it what it is: DEPOSIT, or WITHDRAWAL. If it's a COW, why call it a BOVINE?)

The purpose of this chapter is not to answer all the questions or, for that matter, to ask them. As you proceed through the subsequent essays, some questions, but not all, will be raised and answered. For example, here is a variation on the mysterious numbers of Example 3.

. . . .

Example 4

```
const
    MSG1  = '                     ';
    MSG2  = '***Welcome to System*** ';
    MSG3  = 'Enter User ID:        ';
    MSG4  = 'Id not found          ';
    MSG5  = 'SKIP: skip options    ';
    . . .
    MSG44 = '***Session ended***   ';
type
    DISPLAYMENU = (L11, L12, L13, L14, BLANK, L15, L17);
```

. . . .

The suggestion here is that of a complex problem with a strange solution.

In considering Examples 5 and 6, what questions would you ask? Would you make any inferences about what the rest of the program looks like? Would you be concerned or not? Here one may ask:

- Is compression desirable?
- Should several statements appear on one line?
- When are blank lines effective?
- How helpful are in-line comments?

. . . .

Example 5

```
procedure SETLINES;
    const LINEWIDTH = 72; BLANK = ' '; MIDVAL = 36;
    type LETTER 'A'..'Z';
    var CODELETTER : array[LETTER,LETTER] of LETTER;
        CH1, CH2: CHAR;
        I,J,COUNT: INTEGER;
begin
    for I := 1 to LINEWIDTH do LINE[I] := BLANK;
    writeln('Enter a sequence of lines:');
    READLN(LINE);    COUNT := 0;
    ...
end;
```

Example 6

```
{ Test status of file, and respond }
if OPEN (SFILE)
then

   REPLY := ON
else

  { file closed }
  SET (DISK2);

WRITE ('BLOCKS LOCATED');

{ set block index }
PRG := 16;
CLOSE(DRIVE, 'C');

SETDB('QI14');

if STATUSSWITCH < 0
then
    begin
    ...
```

. . . .

Comment: Some programmers believe that related concepts should be grouped on a single line, say, two constant declarations or two statements. Others, with their attention on program layout itself, insert considerable white space and extensive comments. What do you think?

Now, what's going in Example 7?

. . . .

Example 7

```
procedure COMPARE(LINNUM: INTEGER; ST: MODE);

    var
        FIN: BOOLEAN;
        LINPOS, LINPOS1, LINPOS2: 1 .. 72;
        LIN1, LIN2: STRING;
    begin
      GETFILE1(LIN1);
      GETFILE2(LIN2);
      LINPOS1 := LENGTH(LIN1);
      LINPOS2 := LENGTH(LIN2);

      LINPOS := 0;
      FIN := FALSE;
      while not FIN do
        ...
    end;
```

. . . .

Questions?

- How should one abbreviate?
- Is it better to use abbreviated sequences of two or more words (like LINPOS) or single full words (like POSITION)?

Comment: Somewhere there is a middle ground between programmers who abbreviate to such a degree that three- to six-character names are the rule and programmers who use lengthy full names that get in the way and occupy too much space.

A note on choosing mnemonic names, the mismatch of which can be almost humorous. To wit:

```
if ERROR = NOERROR then
```

The best can be made of this is that ERROR is assumed to be a variable, and NOERROR represents one of the possible enumerated values. What kind of code are we writing if, at any time, we ask any reader to think about the situation where an ERROR is equal to a NOERROR?

Isolated example? Hardly. Consider these:

```
if PLAYER = NONPLAYER then
if ROWNUM = LASTPLAYER then
if COUNT = FIRSTNAME then
```

```
if TABLEPTR = COUNT then
if FIRSTCARD = (LASTCARD - ROW) then
```

None of these Boolean conditions makes any sense. They only beg the question: What really is a good name for _____?

Now look at Example 8. This example contains a good number of global variables (i.e., variables that are declared and used outside the procedure). We have heard that procedures should have relatively few inputs and outputs, and should have one purpose. We all believe in consistency of names. Now is this example a disaster? Or is it really quite acceptable?

Example 8

```
procedure EVENTLOG;
{ This procedure records and controls events into the log. }

    var STATUSNEXT: EVENTREC;

begin
    LOGENTRY := 0;
    CLEARSCREEN;
    MSGAREA := FIELDA;
    NEWAREA := FIELDB;
    DISPLAYBOX(32);
    LOG.COUNT := 0;
    LOG.STATUS := PREVENTSTAT;
    LOG.MSG := BLANKMSG;

while STATUSCOND = CONTINUE do
begin
    FILLBOX(MSGAREA, DIACOUNT, NEWEVENT, EVENTSTATE,
            ITEM, RESULT);
    PROCESSEVENT(NEWEVENT, LOG.STAUS, RTNMSG);
    UPDATELOG(LOG, LOGENTRY, DIACOUNT, EVENTSTATE,
            NEWAREA, NEWDIAG, STATUSNEXT);
    if LOG.STATUS = CLOSED then
        if (LOG.COUNT > 0)
        and (NEWAREA = FIELDC)
        and (STATUSCOND = CONT) then
            LOGENTRY := 99
    else
        SETCONDITION(STATUSNEXT, EVENTSTATE)
    end;

    WRITEBOX('EVENT LOG', 10, 7)
end;
```

And what about the logic? The logic here, first of all, is that the calls to this procedure look innocuously simple. The real complexity at the higher level is manifest at a lower level in the procedure. This is often the case when excessive use of global variables is made. The calls look simple; the procedures themselves suggest otherwise. So the logic probably was a simple idea of a procedure that grew over time to include more. A correction here, another case there, something else to consider over there. Nonetheless, is it acceptable or not?

The moral of all these examples is the same—we need to think about programs. Innocent as we are at the time, when the outside reader looks at the product, he or she may wonder what logic possessed us. The subsequent chapters will examine many day-to-day programming practices.

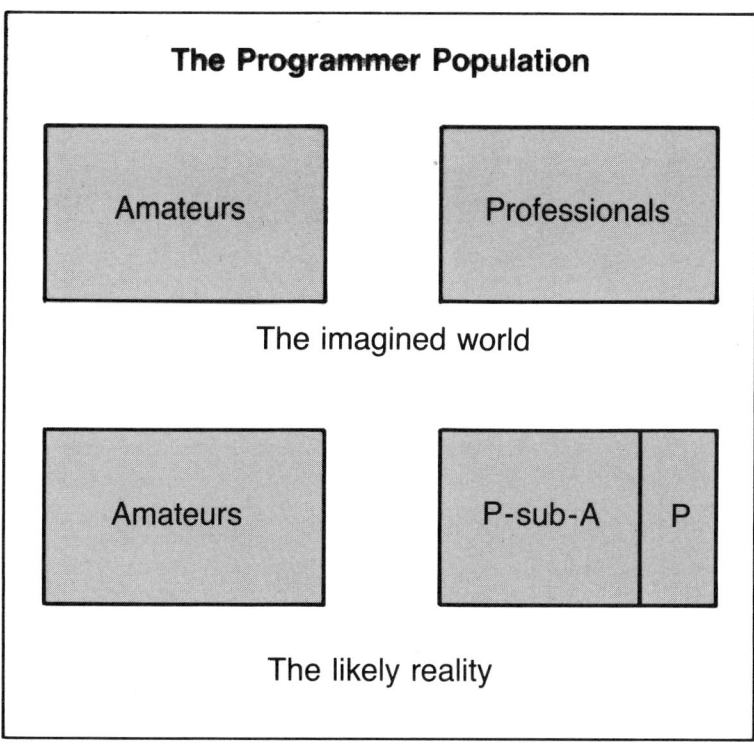

2

Programmers:
The Amateur Versus
The Professional

The Programmer Population

Amateurs

Professionals

The imagined world

Amateurs

P-sub-A   P

The likely reality

At the outset, it should be understood that an endeavor to compare an amateur and a professional does not describe the full hierarchy in programming or any other vocation or avocation. The complete spectrum might be: the ignorant, the novice, the aficionado, the amateur, the professional, and the master.

Music, expressly classical music, comes to mind if all six rankings were to be defined. The novice appreciates Tchaikovsky's 1812 Overture every Fourth of July when the cannons go off along the Charles River in Boston. The novice learns the notes of the scale in order to play an instrument (the guitar, usually). The aficionado can tell the difference between Mozart and Mahler, the amateur can play the first two movements of the "Moonlight" sonata, and the professional can play all 32 Beethoven sonatas. The master writes the music that eventually finds its way into the repertoire.

The distinction between amateur and professional that we are making, however, is probably closer to an analogy with the golfer. Given some basic talent, capable instruction, and a good deal of practice, a young player can approach playing close to par golf and decide to pursue a career as a professional. After a perfunctory declaration or surviving the qualification tournaments, he may end up as a "club pro" or be invited to the Master's Tournament. But his status is clearly defined. What he can or cannot do in golf is limited by his skill. Not so with programmers.

In the past ten years there has been a revolution in the computer industry so that a politician could rightfully campaign for a computer in every home rather than a chicken in every pot. It would be difficult to speculate on how many new computer owners are either ignorant of programming or are novices in the practice. But imagine the delight of the novice when his first program is written:

```
10 REM THIS IS AN ADDING MACHINE
20 LET A = 2
30 LET B = 3
40 LET Y = A + B
50 PRINT Y
```

The answer comes out 5 and a new programmer is born!

So this example is facetious. Perhaps our novice programmer lights onto a program that determines the date of Easter in any year from 1415 to 2030 and is writing a paper on Pope Pius II. Imagine the delight to find that this humanist pope did indeed celebrate Easter Mass on April 19 in 1460, as calculated by the program. Now the novice programmer is almost an amateur.

If at first the computer was a fascination for the very few, it has created a romance that is now a fiber of both industry and academia. No major corporation with even the smallest industrial base can function without a staff of programmers. There is a proliferation of computer courses in colleges and universities across the country. Programming is now even an integral part of high school curricula. In sum, millions of people know how to program to some degree.

A generation of amateur programmers is afoot across the land. And that's all right. Many find programming useful as an addendum to a career in another field, perhaps in biology or management. Often they are good programmers who are not paid primarily for their programming skills. They may indeed be highly skilled in certain aspects of programming and even consider themselves expert programmers.

Those whom we call "professionals" are experienced coders, university graduates, engineers, system developers, computer scientists, or application specialists. They are paid for their computer expertise, which is their specialty. But something has happened. In my view, there are simply too many amateurs today in the professional ranks. Said another way, many programmers have been pushed into professional roles for which they are ill equipped. The problem is compounded in that many of their peers are locked into a purely quantitative practice of programming. The purpose of this work is to define a "professional" as one who has a grasp of the quantitative requirements of this area along with an understanding of the qualitative demands that are necessary to this high calling.

Let us examine these two entities, the amateur and the professional, in their own idealized worlds.

The Amateur

The amateur programmer usually:

1. Writes programs only for a limited number of users;
   a. often only for the author, or
   b. otherwise for a number of colleagues.

2. Writes programs that:
   a. crash under varied and bizarre inputs;
   b. result in unusual but acceptable outputs.

3. Writes programs that only the author needs to be able to read.

4. Writes programs that need not be fully tested.

5. Writes programs that require little documentation.

6. Writes programs without regard to user requirements.

7. Writes programs without regard to some defined software lifecycle (see Figure 2.1 for the "textbook" variant).

8. Writes programs without regard to integration with other, larger, or future systems.

This little taxonomy is not critical, only descriptive of the amateur programmer. Think of the number of calendars our Renaissance historian would have had to count to come up with the date of Easter in 1460. The amateur programmer may be a hobbyist who writes programs to play games or draw pictures, a scientist who writes programs to analyze data, or a university student who writes a program to fulfill a course or thesis requirement. In each case, the programs are written without regard to anyone else having to understand, debug, or maintain them.

A number of issues are unimportant when programs are written for individual use. It doesn't matter if input formats are unwieldy or inconvenient or if the program doesn't work well or all of the time—as long as it works most of the time. These shortcomings are acceptable. What may seem to be bizarre and unusual inputs do not concern the amateur programmer. In writing a program for solving the roots of an equation, for instance, it matters little that someone might enter inputs consisting of carriage returns, people's names, or strange control codes. The amateur knows what the program is supposed to do and these unreasonable inputs seem unreasonable to worry about.

Likewise, the output for the amateur need not be satisfying or pleasing as to format, style, or screen layout. More often than not, the program is used only occasionally and only the programmer needs to understand the output. For example, consider a program designed to compute areas. If measurements are given only to an accuracy of three decimal places, the program might be written using real arithmetic and the output displayed to ten decimal places. To another user of the program this might be annoying, but it does not bother the author. He simply disregards the last seven decimals and presses forward.

For the amateur, the program itself need not be particularly readable. Matters like choosing apropriate names, organizing the program into simple logical units, or giving the program a well-spaced appearance are not of vital concern. Most programmers can read their own programs and fix or debug them when necessary. It's the other person's program that causes trouble.

The amateur seldom has to test a program thoroughly. For the university student, too often the only requirement is to pass stated output requirements in order to pass a course. The fact that most of the control paths have never been exercised is not of much concern in either submitting or planning the program.

Only a few decades ago, almost all programming was done using direct machine codes or assembler language. Placed in the form of a program, these programs were extremely difficult to understand, so getting them to work was a fairly sophisticated task in itself. Sometimes it was almost a miracle when they did work. When they did, there was a great sense of accomplishment in achieving this simple objective. As a result the early days of programming were, by and large, reserved for the elite.

Programming is now widespread in all disciplines and business activities. The mystery and elitism that were understood by a very few have disappeared as programming, in one form or another, has become more critical in our daily activities. Suppose that a corporation develops a piece of software to handle a payroll. Such a program must be written in such a way to have a long life span, and eventually hundreds of people will be involved in simply keeping the program up-to-date with current payroll requirements.

Figure 2.1

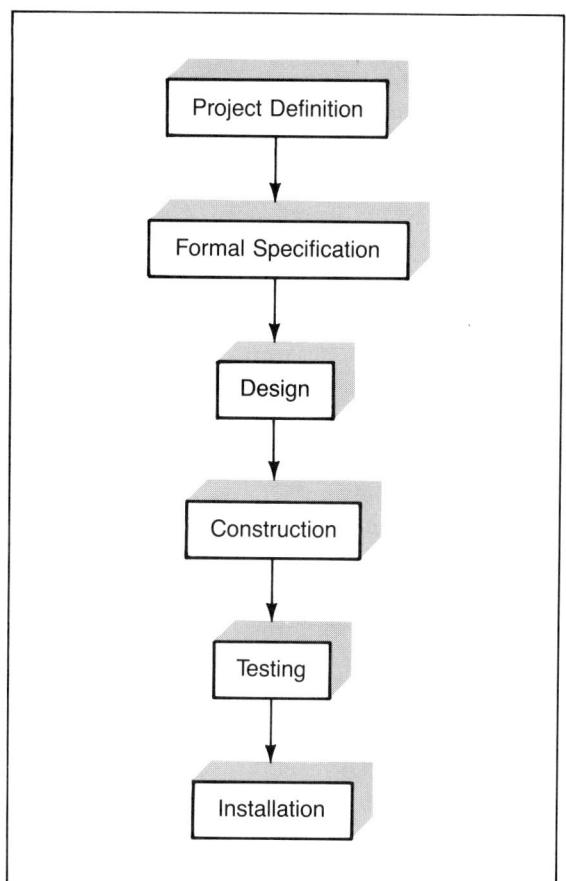

This is a different game than that which an amateur plays. The amateur hardly needs to see what the implications of a program are, how it affects more than just one person, the programmer himself. If the program "does the job," it's all right. If there is any practice that an amateur develops, it is a kind of well-directed tunnel vision for the result: by Jove, it works! And if it works, that's it.

The amateur is not particularly concerned about documenting a program. If the program performs reasonably and the output is fairly consistent, no documentation is required because the program works. No one else has to learn the program, no one else has to maintain it.

And why would an amateur care about the lifecycle of software? The program is the programmer's alone. Any ideas about software specifications are not relevant. User requirements are not a consideration because the programmer is the only user. The requirement is met when the program works, even if the program is fairly complicated. Whatever particular (and personal) needs are required or suggested along the way, the amateur programmer can change the behavior of the program to meet these needs. Features can be added or subtracted along the way. No one else will be affected. If it works out, it's all right.

Any commercially necessary program, such as the payroll program mentioned earlier, has another dimension about it that need not concern the amateur: estimating the resources needed to do the job and estimating the length of time the programming task will take. Of course, the professor meeting a research deadline at the university has some concern for a time schedule. However, the traditional software lifecycle (see Figure 2.1), which includes planning, specification, design, construction, testing, and actual user operation of the program, is hardly relevant and probably a nuisance.

Finally, there is the matter of integrating a program into the software of a larger system. Reasonably, the amateur never considers this in the program design. Creating a generalized sorting package for use inside an operating system or writing a general-purpose formatting program are tasks beyond the desire of the amateur programmer. These kinds of programs must interface with other programs and, in a general sort of way, with the conventions and protocols of the supporting environment. These are the kind of considerations that describe the requirements for any kind of software that is needed, the kind of host for which a program can be written.

If all this describes an idealized world of a skilled amateur programmer, it is simply a world where the programmer is a lone ranger. What of the professional?

The Professional

I quietly suggested earlier that many professionals are amateurs in disguise. This is a more subtle observation than it seems. Paralleling our description of amateur, another shading might be interjected into the spectrum so that we have:

Ignorant
Novice
Aficionado
Amateur
    Amateur who thinks he is a professional
    Amateur who is learning to be a professional
    Professional who is really an amateur
    Professional who didn't quite make it
Professional
Master

The upper-case descriptions are not quite interchangeable, but they exist only at this level of the spectrum. For example, there are no professionals who pose as masters, just as there are few aficionados who presume to be more than intense devotees of the subject. Once again, applying this spectrum to music (and it is just as applicable to any profession), I have a middle-aged friend who is an aficionado of music, who still takes an occasional piano lesson from a professional. But he loves music for the joy of it and doesn't think of himself as an amateur—just as his mentor who holds a chair in a symphony orchestra would not presume to be a master. Both understand, respect, and enjoy their relationship with music.

It is a matter of attitude and status. If we use the symbol P to denote a professional, we could call this new ranking P-sub-A—something between an amateur and a professional. Consider all four shadings:

1. The *amateur who thinks he is a professional* might be a graduate whose knowledge is enough to impress those who are unfamiliar with his profession. Such programmers think they are better than they are. The tragedy, as we shall see, is when this attitude is taken into the marketplace.

2. We must be encouraged by the P-sub-A who is *an amateur who is learning to be a professional.* It is here that we must understand that most professionals were once amateurs, that most of them passed through the P-sub-A phase in their development. I would think that many under-graduate and graduate students are more than amateurs, less than professionals. It's too bad that an old term has passed out of our lexicon—journeyman. It is a much more appealing description, for it implies a positive attitude and a mobile status.

3. The *professional who is really an amateur* is a reflection of status that cements an attitude. Our profession often propels some beyond their capabilities. It is inexpedient to hire new personnel when a familiar hand can be promoted. The requirements of the new post are professional, but the individual has elements of amateur ability. The new status creates (and maybe demands) a professional attitude, but the skills are not all there. Defensiveness and overconfidence set in.

4. The *professional who didn't quite make it* may seem to be a picture of an individual who failed at the heights. But more often than not, especially in our profession, it is a description of one for whom technology has gone too fast or, more likely, one who finally succumbed to unrealistic pressures of management. The problems vary, and there will always be those brief moments of insight that are the hallmark of a professional.

In short, the P-sub-A is in some cases a journeyman, in others he is immobile and likely to remain so. It does not detract, however, from the situation as I have come to understand it. We think (looking upward) that the programming world looks like Figure 2.2a, but my experience has led me to believe that it looks like Figure 2.2b. Many "professionals" are assumed professionals. The true professional is found less often than we think.

Do not take this matter lightly; it is the substance of my arguments. Let me show you why. Figure 2.3 lists some observable characteristics of programmers. You see that we are attempting to define our goal: the description of the *true* professional programmer.

In no way do I wish to suggest here that the professional's task is easy, or even under the professional's control.

1. The project may be so fragmented (Fred's group is doing the user interface; Janet's group, the memory management) that hope for success is dim, diminished at best.

2. The project may be based on a prototype that eventually overwhelms the project.

3. The people involved (management, peers, marketing, support) may exhibit such wide differences that creative skills are nearly impossible to harness.

Perhaps the programmer should quit. Ah, but let us not stray from our course.

Professionals write programs that other people depend on. This could be a piece of software that is commercially available, for example, a program written for a microcomputer in a car, an orbiting satellite, or a mobile telephone unit. It could also be a program that is used to make the monthly billings or schedule courses at a university. The common characteristic of these kinds of programs is that other people make use of the software directly or indirectly. Many users are affected by the programmer's work.

When other people are involved as users, the programmer's task becomes much more difficult. Most software users do not understand the inner workings. They become confused by its operation and are apt to type all sorts of things as inputs into the program. In a word-processing program, if a user is unsure of how to get out of a text-editing mode, for instance, all kinds of consequences can occur. The user can type control codes, carriage returns, file names, and words like "help" or "quit." Even something apparently clear like responding to a computer-prompted question can lead to surprises. The professional must try to account for these spurious cases in writing a program.

Many users demand nearly perfect implementations and are generally impatient with faulty software. The first-time user of a program, especially one who was expecting a Christmas-night reward with a new "toy," may be not only impatient but discouraged: the promises of the program were empty. For the professional programmer, this is a concern at the inception of the program. The software requirements, team composition, attitude toward work, software tools, and schedule—all bear heavily on the ultimate reliability of the program.

Figure 2.2

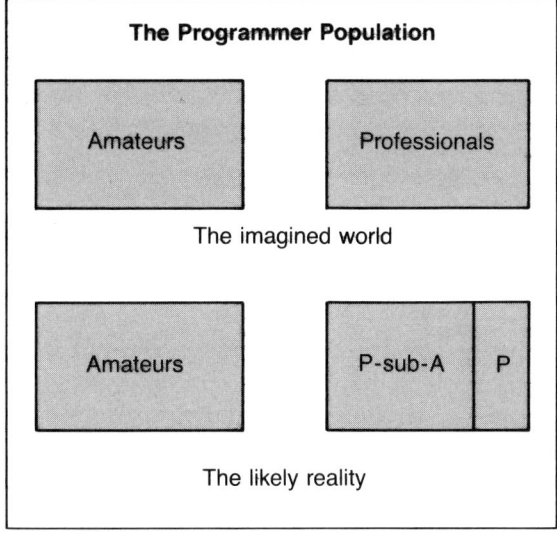

Figure 2.3

Observable Attitudes

The P-sub-A programmer:

1. Perpetuates the mythical user (assumes the user is just like the programmer).

2. Lives in "systems mentality" where dealing with anomalies is a way of life.

3. Considers work reading (that is offering one's own work for open criticism) as a nuisance.

4. Keeps trashing out the bugs.

5. Deals with documentation later.

6. Is always "programming"—always developing some new feature on the terminal.

7. Doesn't see the software lifecycle slowly fall apart.

8. Gets on with the job.

The professional programmer:

1. Writes programs for a large class of users (does *not* assume user knowledge).

2. Worries about "unusual" cases.

3. Writes programs that *anyone* can read.

4. Releases programs with *no* known errors or "strange" features.

5. Writes beautiful documentation *first.*

6. Negotiates and develops user requirements and functional specifications in great detail.

7. Has well-defined phases with hard benchmarks.

8. Writes programs with concern for future and larger systems.

An issue that the amateur almost never considers, but is vital to the professional, is the matter of documentation. Documentation is the means by which other people can specify what the software is to accomplish, a job description, as it were. It is a means to describe one's work to others. There may be preliminary documents describing the intent of the system, project planning, sketches of the technical requirements, user manuals, test data specifications, training guides, and maintenance information. On most projects, these documents are not superfluous. Often they are the cornerstones for defining and measuring progress. For the amateur, a few scruffy pages may seem adequate. For the professional, documentation may consume half of one's working hours.

It is a fallacy to think of documentation as neutral to software behavior. It is not, or at least should not be, an after-the-fact process. Documentation should precede implementation. Written commitments may be needed for a given feature or a given style of behavior. Protocols for the user interface may need to be established. Performance requirements on the speed or use of resources may have to be spelled out. In some cases, the better ones, a preliminary user manual is written before a line of final software is started. Even if the traditional lifecycle model (Figure 2.1) is not used (for instance, basing the project on a prototype), the documentation at least serves as a blueprint for the project.

Professional software must often be integrated with other components of a software or hardware system. A program that handles the management of files in an operating system, for example, must be integrated with the text-editing facilities. This means that the software does not stand alone. In some cases, these concerns can be paramount. Things like protocol for input and output may dictate severe constraints on any supporting software. Often the programmer has no latitude in these matters, but must go to great detail to guarantee that the behavior of software is accurate.

Beyond these more or less technical requirements, there is another issue that *dramatically* distinguishes the professional from the amateur. A professional does not work in isolation. Most professional software projects are simply too big and too extensive for a single person to conceive, write, and maintain.

Projects of the professional dimension have given rise to developing software with a team of participants. Like a professional football team, the professional programming team is a collection of many people who combine many different skills working toward a single goal—a completed software project. Working with others involves many social and organizational aspects. Let me make this one simple point. In many cases, a piece of software may have to be read hundreds of times by many different people before it is publicly released. This puts a responsibility on the author of the program unit. Every minute wasted trying to understand what a particular construct means, every hour wasted wondering how a particular module works, and every day or week wasted when an error is discovered and corrected can result in setbacks for the entire project.

The viability of a general programming effort is hampered by individual idiosyncrasies. The ideas that one has suppressed because of their supposed impotence at first might be the very ones that other team members need to solve a testy problem. Others may make bold talk of their own excellence or think that some completed sub-project is good when it is not. I have observed that such attitudes in software projects are the rule, not the exception. The professional's role is to set exceptionally high standards so that not only does the individual team member understand that all ideas are important, but so that no single team member can consider his or her contribution without fault or criticism.

In some software projects, outside evaluators are called upon to make an independent assessment. This can be a general-purpose review or, later, extensive live testing. The professional welcomes these. A good testing phase is rigorous and thorough. Often the process is automated, in that predefined sets of data are fed to the software. Boundary conditions, spurious inputs, and exceptional cases are all tried.

Professional software is often around for a long time, typically five to ten years. Unlike buying an automobile, the maintenance issue is far more pervasive. There used to be an adage that if you got a "lemon" from Detroit, it was probably a "Monday-morning" car or was built just before new tooling was put on line. Different automobiles may have different maintenance problems, but the software maintenance problem is fundamentally different. Really, for software, "maintenance" is the wrong word.

1. Unlike automobiles, software does not wear out. For given inputs, software continues to produce the same outputs.

2. A sizable part of maintenance goes into altering aspects that were not well designed when the software was initially written. We may later realize that the software takes too much memory, ignores some important case, or crashes under unusual circumstances.

3. Once the software is in use, demands for it change. Yesterday's word processor did not handle footnotes, today's must.

When software goes awry or updates are needed, the authors may have forgotten what was really in the program or may have moved on to other projects. It may be absurd to think that one can find a good mechanic for a 1933 Essex, but one should expect that bugs or updates in a 1983 payroll program can be handled by any good software engineer. Actually, one should expect that there be no bugs at all in the software.

The problem of software produced in a hurry is that maintenance is not a priority in design. Planning for maintenance becomes largely a token homage issue. When things are not quite right, the user is often stuck with a lemon but has no warranty to exercise. On the one hand, overconfident P-sub-A programmers *think* their software is maintainable; on the other, most of them complain about the "other person's" software they are assigned to maintain. Quite simply, maintainable software is seldom written.

This problem becomes apparent to software customers when they find a new version coming out every year or so. It's the software counterpart of a Detroit recall of automobiles. "We found out something didn't work out the first time—we hope you like it better the second time around." Why should a user want a new release of an old program? Why wasn't the software right in the first place? What does one do with the old manuals? Of course, there may be solid reasons for a particular case, but I often have doubts.

In short, consider a final comparative of our P-sub-A and the professional:

Observable Attitudes

The P-sub-A programmer: *The professional programmer:*

9. Writes software for the computer.   9. Writes software for the human reader.

. . . .

For the P-sub-A programmer, the human reader is an aside. For the true professional, the computer is only a necessary prerequisite. The human reader is paramount.

The world of the amateur and the professional are strikingly different. So, too, are the worlds of the assumed professional (P-sub-A) and the true professional. These differences are observable. Ultimately the differences are manifest in the *quality* of their work.

Part One

Programming Practice

The Naming Thicket

Programmer's Thesaurus

815. SIZE

1. GENERIC NAMES. *Size*, *Length*, Width, Height, Capacity, Content, Extent, Magnitude, Area, *Sum*

2. NOUNS. *Count*, *Index*, *I*, Number, N, *Num*, Order, NumInHand, Quantity, Score, Tally, Amount

3. ABBREVIATIONS. *I*, *Num*, *N*, J, K, Num1, Num2, X (for real variables), Y (for real variables), Qty, Amt

4. PROCEDURES. *GetSize*, GetLength, *ReadSize*, ReadLength, etc. Also ComputeSize, DetermineSize, GenerateSize, EstimateSize, ObtainSize

817. STORAGE

1. GENERIC NAMES. *Buffer*, Array, *Table*, Stack, Stove, Reserve, Area, TempArea, List, Listing, *File*, Space, Storage, Storage Space, Data Area,

2. GENERIC VERBS. *Store*, Put, Get, Hold, Log, *Save*, Keep, Record, Post, *File*, Update

3. SPECIFIC NAMES. InBuffer, OutBuffer, Item, Table, ValueArray, ValueTable, etc. NewValueStack, PointerArray, ElementList, IntFile, . . .

Programmers must choose names (identifiers) for the objects in a program. If you write a procedure to perform some calculation, you must give the procedure a name. If you have a record type to denote the items in a collection of data, you must give the type a name. If you have a variable or a constant that denotes some value, you must give the constant or variable a name. This is the issue of naming, a difficult issue in writing programs.

Let us start with a contrived example:

```
program LINES (INPUT, OUTPUT);

    { -- This program is deliberately misleading. }

    var
        DEL1, DEL2, DEL3, DEL4: INTEGER;
        A, B, C: array[1..2] of INTEGER;

begin
    READ (A[1], B[1], C[1], A[2], B[2], C[2]);
    DEL1 := B[1] - A[1];
    DEL2 := C[1] - A[1];
    DEL3 := B[2] - A[2];
    DEL4 := C[2] - A[2];
    if (DEL1 * DEL4) = (DEL2 * DEL3) then
        WRITELN ('YES')
    else
        WRITELN ('NO')
end.
```

This example performs a computation that is familiar to most high school students. Each variable name is just enough off track so that the collection of names as a whole is not at all clear. The program is a mystery.

Next look at the following procedure header:

```
WRDISPLAYREC (SQDESIG: POSITION);
```

The intent of this procedure is to display a particular item at a given position on a screen. The letters WR presumably stand for "write". Yet following it is the word "display". This is a kind of double-talking. The word "display" would be sufficient. The suffix REC presumably stands for "record" or "rectangle." It appears quite superfluous to the meaning. Notice also that SQDESIG is specified as of type POSITION. This naming is somewhat awkward. Presumably SQDESIG stands for a square designation. A simpler and probably clearer rendering of this header might be

```
DISPLAYSQ (SQ: POSITION);
```

Next consider a simple pair of procedure calls

```
COORDINATE (PIECE, XPOS, YPOS);
GETPIECE (PIECE, COLOR);
```

The first call presumably gets the X and Y positions of a given piece, and the second call gets the color of a designated piece. Note that the first procedure is designated by a noun and the second procedure by a verb phrase. The second procedure is entitled GETPIECE and yet the item returned by the procedure is not in fact a piece, but a color. The procedure is misnamed. This simple sequence would be better rendered as

```
GETCOORD (PIECE, XPOS, YPOS);
GETCOLOR (PIECE, COLOR);
```

The kind of confusion in these rather simple examples is just the beginning. Such problems can easily destroy the workings of any program. In fact, like many other issues in programming, programmers generally pay some attention to the issue of naming, but never realize the deeper implications involved. The issue of naming also falls into my category of token homage issues. Let us look at the matter more closely.

The Goal

In a more realistic setting, consider:

```
{ - Code to test legality of a move }
if (STATUSARRAY[NUM1] = PLAYERPIECE)
and (STATUSARRAY[NUM2] = EMPTY) then begin
   ONJUMP := FINDJUMP(STATUSARRAY, COLOR);

   if ONJUMP then
      begin
         if (LEFTJUMPTABLE[COLOR, NUM1] = NUM2)
         or (RIGHTJUMPTABLE[COLOR, NUM1] = NUM2) then
            TESTMIDSQ(NUM1, NUM2, STATUS)
      end
   else
      if (LEFTMOVES[COLOR, NUM1] = NUM2)
      or (RIGHTMOVES[COLOR, NUM1] = NUM2) then
         STATUS = OKMOVE
end;
```

What is wrong here? Nothing? No. This is P-sub-A code.

- NUM1 and NUM2 are numbers, yes, but *square* numbers in particular.

- STATUSARRAY is really a representation of a *checkerboard*.

- The statement ONJUMP := FINDJUMP(. . .) reads in a very odd fashion, English-wise.

- FINDJUMP does not *find* a jump.

- The COLOR (red or black) is the color of a *player*.

- The array names LEFTMOVES and RIGHTMOVES should not be plural; they do not denote moves, but *squares*.

- The suffix TABLE in LEFTJUMPTABLE is confusing.

- The name STATUS is too broad.

- OKMOVE is awkward to read.

You see the nature of reading programs is thwarted by names that, when read, have no *natural* counterpart in the problem domain.

This leads me to a broad strategy for choosing names:

1. Select a section of code in which one or more names are used intensively.

2. Write this section.

3. Pick names so that this section reads easily and coherently in the *problem* domain.

Note: If *C* is a concept or item we wish to name and *N* is a name, the game is *not*

Does *C* imply *N?*

(which is where programmers err), but

Does *N* imply *C?*

This goal is:

The code should flow, effortlessly.

Let me show an alternative to the fragment on checkers:

```
{ -- Code to test legality of a move }
if (BOARD[SQ1] = PLAYERSPIECE)
and (BOARD[SQ2] = VACANT) then begin
   if JUMPAVAILABLE(BOARD, PLAYER) then
      begin
         if (LEFTJUMPSQ [PLAYER, SQ1] = SQ2)
         or (RIGHTJUMPSQ[PLAYER, SQ1] = SQ2) then
            TESTMIDSQ(SQ1, SQ2, MOVESTATUS)
      end
```

```
    else
        if (LEFTSQ [PLAYER, SQ1] = SQ2)
        or (RIGHTSQ[PLAYER, SQ1] = SQ2) then
            MOVESTATUS := MOVEOK
    end;
```

This is a solid step forward in readability.

Having stated the goal, let us look at some of the pieces of this naming puzzle.

Accuracy

The first, and by far most important, issue is the accuracy of the name itself. This matter itself is complex and difficult.

Let us start by picking some names out of the hat. Remember to ask, "What does the name imply?" One of the most common variable names in programming is the name COUNT. Immediately we would expect COUNT to denote a quantity that

1. Is updated during runtime, and
2. Represents a positive whole number.

For example, we would certainly be surprised if COUNT were of type REAL. We would also be surprised to find that COUNT were declared as a constant, or even worse, if COUNT were declared as a record or a Boolean variable. The point here is that such uses are counter to our expectations (see "psychological set" in Weinberg, 1971).

Now let us pick another name, IDNUM. To start with we would expect this name to be an abbreviation for the concept of an identification number. We might expect to find such a name as part of a record structure or to see a sorted list of such values. On the other hand, we would be surprised to see a statement adding values to IDNUM. We have no particular concept of arithmetic with identification numbers. They are passive values that denote a number associated with an individual or object.

Now let us look at the name GETLINE. It is the verb "get" followed by the noun "line". Thus we would expect this name to denote a procedure, in particular, a procedure that obtains a line of text or a line of data from some input device. We would be quite surprised to find the name declared as a variable.

To show the diffuseness of this issue, consider Table 3.1. The point of these little examples is that, when we see a name in a program, we draw a number of immediate conclusions about what the name should mean. Names have many connotations, and ensuring that these expectations are met is a primary ingredient in writing clear programs.

Table 3.1 *What's in a Name*

RMS2	This name appears odd, but is conceivable. At the very least we would expect there to be another variable called RMS1. Moreover, we would expect the initials R, M, and S to be an abbreviation for something, most likely a sequence of three words like "Remote Monitor Switch" or "Root Mean Square".
X, Y	A likely expectation is that X and Y denote the coordinates on a grid system or the roots in an equation. We would be surprised if they stored temporary values or if X had no relationship to Y.
FLAG	We would certainly expect this variable to be of type BOOLEAN and denote some program status. We would be surprised if the variable denoted an integer quantity or if it were the name of a procedure. Otherwise we are left guessing. The name gives little idea as to what the flag is supposed to flag.
EXITPOINT	This name suggests a label prefixing some final statement in a program. One might question whether the name POINT is truly accurate. The name is a bit of a mystery, although one might imagine cases (e.g., a game playing program) where the name might be good.
INVALID	The word is an English adjective, and would most likely be associated with a status value. If the name denoted an invalid character code, for instance, we might get confused since the name itself is an adjective and does not suggest a noun value.
TAXARRAY	This is jargon. Most real-world applications involving taxes have little to do with arrays, at least as far as the user is concerned. The name TAXTABLE might be preferable.
A,B,C	These are beautiful names for the coefficients in a quadratic equation.
TEMP	This is a faceless name. It could stand for a temporary value or a temperature. Except for a faceless value, it gives little clue as to what the value is.
TERM	This is a loaded name. It could stand for an academic school year, a member of a series, a syntactic category, a terminal, etc.
COL	This name had better denote a column and not a row. It should not denote an arbitrary index or an arbitrary pointer value. This little name is often abused, but when, for instance, it stands for a particular column in a table or a line of text, it can be just right.

In choosing a name, one simple rule has often served me in good stead. It stems from conventional English and goes as follows:

Variables	should be denoted by	*Nouns*
Procedures	should be denoted by	*Verbs* (or verb phrases)
Booleans	should be denoted by	*Adjectives*

The reasons here are quite simple. Variables have a value, and most often, values are quantities denoted by nouns. Procedures denote actions, and actions are normally denoted by verbs or verb phrases. Boolean values denote the status or condition and these can be conveniently described by adjectives.

For example, the names LINENUM, ROOT1, RUNNINGTOTAL, BOARD, and ITEMTABLE are perfectly good variable names. GETLINE, COMPUTE-TOTAL, SETFLAGS, and MOVELEFT are perfectly good procedure names. BUSY, ACTIVE, and BUFFERFULL are perfectly good Boolean names. The rule need not be hard and fast, but it is a good general guideline in the choice of names.

Context

The meaning suggested by a name is quite dependent on its context. Thus context can allow us to choose names that are *shorter* than would otherwise be required. For example, the name TOTAL, when appearing in code fragment that has something to do with test scores, might be a reasonable choice for a variable denoting the total score.

Consider:

```
NEWNODE  := TREEROOT;
while (NEWNODE <> EMPTYNODE) and (not NODEFOUND) do begin
    if SEARCHVALUE < NEWNODE.KEYVALUE then
        NEWNODE := NEWNODE@.LEFTBRANCH
    else if SEARCHVALUE > TREENODE.KEYVALUE then
        NEWNODE := NEWNODE@.RIGHTBRANCH
    else
        NODEFOUND := TRUE
end;
```

This little fragment is fairly clear. Nonetheless, it is about searching nodes in a tree. This is clear to *any* serious reader. We can use this general context to shorten the choice of names. Consider now the following rendering:

```
NODE := ROOT;
while (NODE <> EMPTYNODE) and (not KEYFOUND) do begin
    if SEARCHVALUE < NODE.KEY then
        NODE := NODE@.LEFT
    else if SEARCHVALUE > NODE.KEY then
        NODE := NODE@.RIGHT
    else
        KEYFOUND := TRUE
end;
```

This, I suggest, is more potent. The context helps us avoid the tedium of giving names that are excessive and burdensome both to write and to read.

Context, however, is not without its price. We must be consistent. If we are writing a program to monitor input data, for example, it is quite confusing to see a character buffer denoted by different names in different parts of the program. We should not use, say, the variable name BUFFER and later use the name CHARBUFFER or CHARBUFF. If we are writing a program to read in lines of text and we need to denote the particular position on the line, it is not helpful to use the name POSITION in one place and later use the names COL, INDEX, I, POS, or PTR. If we are doing a payroll calculation, it is confusing to in one place use the name HOURS and later use the name NUMHOURS, NUMHRS, HRS, or NHOURS. This little point may sound perfectly obvious, but it is rare to see it done well.

The problem here is a matter of local standardization. The application area determines a name space of items that are frequently used. It requires some discipline and some management to choose and administer consistent names, but the gains are always worth it.

Abbreviation

I now turn to an issue that is always problematic—abbreviation. Good short names are better than good long names. Lengthy names are a bane to the programmer and to the reader; lines become excessively long, parameter lists get unwieldy to read, output statements become cumbersome, and expressions become difficult to parse. On the other side, if we abbreviate too much, the central goal, that of meaning, is lost. The general dilemma is the conflict between brevity and clarity.

There are hazards in choosing abbreviations. The most notorious is making abbreviations so short that names almost become puzzles. Names like RMS2, CURSORRL, NP, PPPSTATUS, and the like can become quite a challenge to decipher. The programmer may know exactly what is intended, but except in the most rigid of circumstances, such names can readily baffle the reader. At the least, abbreviations should be long enough to suggest their original meaning.

Another hazard is a name that stumbles over itself. Examples like

```
NOITEM, STENTRY, TXAMT, FSTONL, and LNINC
```

are troublesome. The fact that these names stand for the number of an item, a statement entry, a tax amount, the first on a list, and a line increment is not of much help when reading the names in a program. It would be better to be a bit more cautious and use names like

```
NUMITEMS, ENTRYOFSTM, TAXAMT, FIRSTONLIST, and LINEINC.
```

Even better, it is reasonable in these circumstances to rethink our general naming strategy.

There is also a danger when different abbreviations with similar spellings are used in the same context. For instance, consider

CURSORUD	meaning	CURSOR Up Down
CURSORDU	meaning	CURSOR Down Up
CURSORLR	meaning	CURSOR Left Right
CURSORRL	meaning	CURSOR Right Left

This simple naming convention can be used by an unsuspecting programmer to indicate the valid directions for moving a cursor. A simple mistake, like CURSORLR in place of CURSORRL, can result in a runtime error that is almost impossible to find. More importantly, the problem with names like these is that they result in a general confusion. Constant attention is needed to focus on what the individual names stand for.

Abbreviated names can also create odd problems:

STATUS.MESS := TRUE;	MESSage
FIND := 1;	FirstINDex
procedure CMPLNS;	unpronounceable

Here we have

1. A shortened name (MESS) that has a totally different connotation on its own.

2. A shortened compound name (FIND) that does not convey its constituent parts.

3. A shortened name (CMPLNS) that is unpronounceable.

It is surprising how these odd names creep in.

One of the best strategies for abbreviations, which unfortunately is not always possible, is to use standard dictionary abbreviations for common words. For example, HRS is a fine abbreviation for HOURS, AMT is a fine abbreviation for AMOUNT, INC is a fine abbreviation for increment, and so on. Where standard abbreviations exist, they .are almost always superior to the longer version.

Unfortunately these common abbreviations are not enough. A wise recourse is to adopt some standard abbreviations for a given project. Consider the following list.

AVE	for AVERAGE
CHAR	for CHARACTER
IN	for INPUT
MAX	for MAXIMUM
MIN	for MINIMUM
MSG	for MESSAGE

```
NUM     for NUMBER
OUT     for OUTPUT
POS     for POSITION
PTR     for POINTER
RPT     for REPORT
SQ      for SQUARE
STR     for STRING
```

These words will often form parts of longer names and can be used to make life a lot nicer, for example, using

```
AVE,      RUNNINGAVE
IDNUM,    PARTNUM
BOARDRPT, SUMMARYRPT
SQNUM,    NEWSQ
OLDCHAR,  NEXTCHAR
INFILE,   INVALUE
OUTFILE,  OUTVALUE
```

The name

```
GETCHARPOS
```

is certainly better than

```
GETCHARACTERPOSITION
```

Every project should have such a list of abbreviations.

But now, watch for the fine print. If possible, even the use of abbreviations should be avoided. Why? Whole words are clearer than abbreviated words. How? Rely on context, using different words, and thinking. Full words are not always optimal, but look again at

```
GETCHARPOS
```

It *may* be obvious that this procedure is about characters, and the name

```
GETPOSITION
```

may be perfect. Also consider:

```
QUOTIENTVAL  vs.  QUOTIENT      ("value" may not be important)
RUNNINGAVE   vs.  AVERAGE       ("running" might be assumed)
CARDDECK     vs.  DECK          (decks always have cards)
EXCESSCHARS  vs.  EXCESS        (if only about characters)
NUMVOWELS    vs.  COUNT         (if only about vowels)
CURRINDENT   vs.  INDENTATION   (there may be only one)
```

In these cases the names on the right may be superior. This issue is not easy, but at least sets a goal, which the programmer must balance against other goals.

Magic Constants

Another issue that gets some but not enough attention is the use of mysterious or "magic" constants, for instance, fragments like

```
a.  LINE[72] := EOLNMARK

b.  FILLPAGE (LINE, 66)

c.  if (WIDTH > MAXWIDTH) then
        ERROR := 34

d.  CONTRIBUTIONS := (GROSSPAY * 0.01) + (BONUS * 0.10)

e.  for I := 1 to 20 do
        PROCESSMATRIX (MATRIX1)

f.  if (FIRSTCHAR = '$') then
        GETCOMMAND(LINE, ENDPOSITION)
```

The problem here is that many readers do not know what 34, 0.01, 72, and so forth mean. Even in the last example, the meaning of the dollar sign character is a touch mysterious, similar to a magic number.

Magic constants can easily be eliminated by the use of enumeration literals and named constants. For instance, with the declarations

```
const
    LINESPERPAGE  = 66;
    MAXLINELENGTH = 72;
    COMMANDCHAR   = '$';
    ...


type
    ERRORNAME = (INVALIDID, INVALIDNUM, LONGLINE, ...);
```

the preceding examples can be written

```
a.  LINE[MAXLINELENGTH] := EOLNMARK

b.  FILLPAGE (LINE, LINESPERPAGE)

c.  if WIDTH > MAXWIDTH then
        ERROR := LONGLINE

d.  CONTRIBUTIONS := (GROSSPAY * POLITICALRATE) + (BONUS * CHARITYRATE)

e.  for I := I to NUMITERATIONS do
        PROCESSMATRIX(MATRIX1)
```

```
f.  if (FIRSTCHAR = COMMANDCHAR) then
        GETCOMMAND(LINE, ENDPOSITION)
```

The rule here is that when a number or symbol has a meaning beyond its literal value (it is senseless to name 0 as ZERO), the value should be named.

Declaring Names

Finally, a point about declarations. The first encounter with the names in a program usually happens in the sections where the names are declared. All too often, names are grouped in a rather ad hoc fashion.

Consider the fragment:

```
var
    SENSOR, COMMANDSIZE, PORT1, PORT2, LIMIT,
    DURATION, CLOCK, BUFFER, INCODE, INTERRUPT,
    OUTCODE, IOSTATUS, ARGUMENT, ERRORCODE,
    INVALUE, COUNT: INTEGER;

    TEMPERATURE, ALTITUDE, HOLDER, APPROX, BOUND,
    DISTANCE, SENSORVALUE, OUTVALUE: REAL;

    COMMAND, OPTION, ERRORNAME: SYMBOL;

    BLOCKED, COMMANDMODE, BUFFERFULL, ERRORFLAG,
    TIMEOUT, LIMITEXCEEDED: BOOLEAN;
```

This kind of name blitz is found over and over again in P-sub-A code. I have seen cases where the collection is many times longer than even this fragment.

The problem here is the lack of discrimination to aid the reader who needs to check the declarations. In the preceding example, it is the commonality of syntax (for example, listing all integer variables in one place) that drives the organization. Consider instead the following rendering of the same declarations. Here the related names are grouped by meaning.

```
var
    SENSOR, PORT1, PORT2,
    INTERRUPT, COUNT,
    ERRORCODE: INTEGER;

    SENSORVALUE: REAL;
    LIMITEXCEEDED, BLOCKED: BOOLEAN;

    TEMPERATURE, ALTITUDE, DISTANCE: REAL;
```

```
INCODE, INVALUE: INTEGER;
BOUND, HOLDER, APPROX,
OUTVALUE: REAL;

BUFFER: INTEGER;
BUFFERFULL: BOOLEAN;

DURATION, LIMIT,
CLOCK: INTEGER;
TIMEOUT: BOOLEAN;

COMMAND, OPTION, ERRORNAME: SYMBOL;
COMMANDMODE, ERRORFLAG: BOOLEAN;
COMMANDSIZE, ARGUMENT: INTEGER;
```

Or, in a more column-like format, we could write

```
var
    SENSOR,
    PORT1, PORT2,
    COUNT,
    INTERRUPT,
    ERRORCODE: INTEGER;

    SENSORVALUE: REAL;
    LIMITEXCEEDED,
    BLOCKED: BOOLEAN;
      .   .   .
```

With the revised renderings we see even more clearly that something should be done about the names themselves. Here the only point I wish to make is that some reasonable organization is needed. It doesn't matter if we have a list of constants, variables, types, or procedures. My own preference is grouping by meaning.

Escaping the Thicket

Our discourse on names has been intricate. Some recommendations along the way were:

- Place accuracy first!

- Head for brevity.

- Use nouns (or noun phrases) for variables, verbs (or verb phrases) for procedures.

- Name mysterious constants.
- Always ask what a name suggests on its own, not whether this is a good name for "...".
- Use abbreviation if necessary.
- Use context to shorten names.
- Do not abbreviate names for unusual items and concepts.

All of these are intended to serve the following broad goal:

Try to make the code speak for itself, effortlessly.

4

Comments:
The Reader's Bridge

. . . .

```
[      This program performs arithmetic on fractions. All fractions
computed to the lowest common denominator. It prints results in fr
form. A fraction is denoted by a positive integer without a sign,
by a slash, and another positive unsigned integer. These fractions
combined in general arithmetic expressions using the conventional
operators. As is the normal convention, multiplication and divisi
precedence over addition and subtraction.
       The program uses several key variables in performing its co
The first is CURRENTVAL. This variable holds the current value c
for the expression. Intermediate values are stored on a stack na
STACKOFVALS. This stack is maintained during the course of the
computation, and a pointer to its current depth (STACKPTR) spec
number of items currently in the stack. The maximum stack depth
entries. During the course of the computation, a number of err
arise. These include expressions that are not well-formed arit
expressions, the use of symbolic names in expressions (which a
allowed), and the use of numbers with decimal points.
       The main program calls three procedures. The first is GE
This procedure gets the next expression from the user of the
handles the interaction with the user. The second procedure
This procedure takes the string of characters given as input
it according to the noraml rules of fractional arithmetic. T
procedure, called PRINTRESULT, prints the result of the comp
of the various procedures can result in the reporting of on
errors.
       The program can handle successive arithmetic expressio
input one at a time from the user as the user sees fit. Wh
decides that enough expressions have been entered, the use
the program once and for all by entering the word STOP in
expression.
```

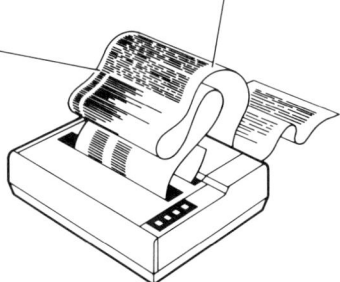

Seemingly mundane events in the newspaper can demonstrate how computer programming affects our future life. Mrs. Emma McFee passed on at the age of 93; her late husband was a former trust officer of the Kowloon Savings Bank in Hong Kong. In this case, the British concluded a treaty with The People's Republic of China on turning over Hong Kong to the Chinese in 1999. McFee's estate includes a substantial holding in Hong Kong municipal bonds with a maturity date of 2015.

What to do? Or better, what has been done? Somewhere, someone may be reading a computer printout that has projections for the prospects of investment in the post-British environment of Hong Kong. The program for these projections have been written so that the results might be:

a. Sell your Hong Kong holdings before January, or
b. Buy Hong Kong dollars as fast as you can now.

Simple as the printout might be for the executor of Mrs. McFee's estate, those projections are probably filled with more calculations than the executor could imagine. And along with the code of the program itself, there may be enough comments to expand it needlessly, or there may be barely any comments at all.

In several years especially if a new regime in China has different thoughts, new calculations may have to be put into the projections for future investment in Hong Kong. The reader of the program will probably not be the author of the program. Scanning a program written years before and having new projections to add, the programmer will have to revise the program and be guided by the original author's comments that he finds there. Will he be able to revise the program or even have some idea of how the program works in the first place?

Initially, a comment may serve to remind the programmer of where he is or where he is going—this is especially useful for the amateur programmer. For example, to elaborate his new found adding machine, the amateur programmer might write:

```
10   REM THIS IS AN ADDING MACHINE
20   LET A = 2
30   LET B = 3
40   LET Y = A + B
50   PRINT Y
60   REM NOW MAKE A MULTIPLICATION MACHINE
70   LET Z = A*B
80   PRINT Z
90   REM THIS IS FUN
```

So we are being facetious again. Here the comments are not inspiring. They only remind the amateur of the obvious.

It surprises me that there are so few research articles on comments in programs, yet programmers put comments in their programs all the time. Some programs contain more comments than lines of code; others have no comments.

Does it matter? Some programmers are told to make their programs "self-documenting" and they take that to mean: make plenty of comments. Some assembler programs have a comment on every line. In some Pascal programs, there is a comment after each variable in a variable declaration. Are these good ideas?

There is so much confusion about comments in programming that it is difficult to know where to start. But I begin with this observation: in my experience (from the numerous pieces of code that I have seen, code written mostly by P-sub-A professionals), 80 percent of the comments are rubbish. Most comments ought not to have been put into the program in the first place. I hope to justify this observation here.

Some Broad Principles

The professional thinks of a comment as a way to proceed from one point (a given state of knowledge) to another (understanding what is written in the program). The professional writes comments that assume something about the reader of the program in the future—the reader being someone other than himself.

It is fair to assume that the reader of a program knows the language in which the program is written. The reader's difficulty is to modify the program at hand.

I have met few programmers who pay attention to comments. Readers of a program are generally interested in the program itself. Comments are only inserted to aid the comprehension of the program—they have no intrinsic value in themselves. This suggests that comments should be visually separated from the program itself so that it is possible to read the program directly and ignore the comments. The person who, in effect, is working in a maintenance environment years after the program is written will be able to revise the program without being distracted by the comments or having the comments intrude upon the work.

A program is in some sense a permanent object in that it can have a long lifetime. For the projections about Hong Kong, the program should last as long as the rules of economics remain the same and both the Chinese and British governments abide (more or less) by their prior agreements. For the future reader, comments in a program should be *truly* substantive. Too many P-sub-A programmers have a tendency to dribble on, to ignore good presentation, to concentrate on minor aspects of the program, and to avoid the more difficult aspects that really deserve comments. Comments in a program should say something. They should assist the program reader.

These observations lead to some specific recommendations. First, regarding the idea of comments as a bridge in programming:

- Extensive comments at the beginning of a program are entirely in order.

These comments set the stage for reading the program. They may contain an outline of the solution adopted by the programmer, summarize its inputs and outputs, give a directory of key variable names, or describe an algorithm that may not be known to the reader. Such comments provide a direct bridge from the problem to the program. They do not intrude on the reading of the program itself because they appear at the beginning of the program and can be read or not as the reader desires.

A second recommendation has to do with procedures and other major subunits of the program.

- Comments should be put at the beginning of each unit.

For example, comments following a procedure header explaining the general nature of the procedure are not only in order but may be necessary. Keeping in mind the bridge aspect, we need not describe the calling environment. The professional assumes that the reader has penetrated the program to such a degree that the procedure calls are understood—but maybe, not the procedure itself. As such, the procedure header comments should be short and help the reader understand the *next* level of detail in the program.

Third, the professional should spend the most energy on the code itself. This means:

- Avoid embedded (in-line) comments within the body of the program itself.

I admit that this is a rather controversial position, but it is my view that such comments can readily intrude upon the meaning of a program. Ideally, the code should speak for itself and require few supporting comments.

Annotating the Obvious

One culprit is the use of comments to annotate things that are quite self-explanatory. For the amateur, we can see something like

```
{ Variable declarations }
var
   UPPER, LOWER,
   INDEX, COUNT: INTEGER;
   . . .
```

It would be hard to find any serious reader of a program who could benefit from this comment. In a textbook illustrating Pascal constructs, fine; but in a professional program, hardly.

Another example of wasted comments arises in annotating variable names that really stand for themselves. Consider the following:

```
var
   LINE: INPUTLINE;      { -- A line of text }
```

```
COL,                    { -- A column position }
CURRENTCOL: COLNUM;     { -- The current column }
LEFTINDENT: INTEGER;    { -- Number of spaces on left }
```

The variable names and associated type names need little amplification. These comments do not serve a useful purpose.

The issue of annotating the obvious, however, can get more subtle. Consider the following example:

```
{ -- Print results }
WRITELN (BLANK:5, TABLEHEADING);
WRITELN;
for I := 1 to TABLESIZE do begin
   WRITELN(BLANK:5, MIDVALUE[I]:10, RESULTVALUE[I]:10);
   WRITELN
end;
CLOSE (INFILE)
```

The issue here is whether the comment actually helps. My own belief is that it is not particularly helpful, although good professional programmers might disagree. The names TABLEHEADING and RESULTVALUE suggest that results are the objects of interest, and the calls to WRITELN also suggest that concern is with output. It could be argued that the comment summarizes the meaning of the seven lines of code. In this instance, it may suggest that the code itself is part of a larger routine that has some larger purpose. This, in turn, suggests that the code might be better as a procedure. The preceding code could be replaced with the call

```
PRINTRESULTS (MIDVALUE, RESULTVALUE)
```

Here there is clearly no need for a comment because the procedure name serves precisely as a comment.

Next consider

```
procedure GETROOTS (A, B, C: REAL;
                    var X1, X2: REAL);

{ -- This procedure finds the roots of a quadratic equation. }
```

This comment gives a piece of information that is not conveyed in the procedure header, namely, that the roots are that of a quadratic equation. If conveying this fact is at all important, the procedure name could be as

```
procedure GETQUADRATICROOTS (A, B, C: REAL;
                             var X1, X2: REAL);
```

Again, if possible, the code should always speak for itself.

Even a long-winded name like GETQUADRATICROOTS is not really a full solution. More often, procedures deserve a good comment of their own. For the example of quadratic roots, we might remind the reader what the quadratic equation is or describe what happens if certain boundary conditions or exceptional conditions are not satisfied. A better rendering of the preceding example might be:

```
procedure GETROOTS (A, B, C: REAL;
                     var X1, X2: REAL);


{ -- Store in X1 and X2 the two roots of a quadratic equation
           Ax**2 + Bx + C = 0.0
  -- If A is zero or there are no real roots, X1 and X2 are left
  -- unchanged and a diagnostic message is printed. }
```

A few lines like this can often help the reader cross the bridge. The goal is content and precision, not words.

Consider now the following example:

```
procedure GETNEXTARRIVAL (D: DISTRIBUTION;
                          var T: TIME);


{ -- This procedure gets the next arrival time. }
```

Here we have an amateurish comment describing what is obvious from the procedure header itself. Those who are enamored with comments can often make a situation worse. Consider the following rendering:

```
procedure GETNEXTARRIVAL (D: DISTRIBUTION;
                          var T: TIME);


{ -- This procedure determines the next arrival time.
  -- It uses a random number to determine the exact arrival.
  -- The distribution of arrival times D is taken from a simulation.
  -- The arrival time T is given as a result. }
```

This comment is not too long but hardly sparks much interest. The first sentence says that the procedure is about getting the arrival times. This is obvious from the header. The second sentence mentions that arrival times are chosen at random. In simulation programs, this is probably obvious too. The third sentence doesn't say much, and the last sentence states the obvious.

To keep the same level of detail and yet improve the situation, I suggest that the following is all that is needed:

```
procedure GETNEXTARRIVAL ({using}  D: DISTRIBUTION;
                          {giving} var T: TIME);
```

The two little comments "using" and "giving" convey essential information at minimal verbosity.

Marker Comments

The last example brings up a point that I have often found useful. Consider the following procedure heading:

```
procedure CHECKLINE (LINE: STRING; LINELENGTH: INTEGER;
                     STR: STRING; STRLENGTH: INTEGER;
                     var FOUND: BOOLEAN; var STARTPOS: INTEGER);
```

This is a familiar but uninspiring way to present procedure headings, typical of the style of a P-sub-A programmer. There is little attempt to distinguish the roles of the various parameters. Now consider the following rendering:

```
procedure CHECKLINE ({inputs}  LINE:           STRING;
                                LINELENGTH:     INTEGER;
                                STR:            STRING;
                                STRLENGTH:      INTEGER;
                     {outputs}  var FOUND:      BOOLEAN;
                                var STARTPOS:   INTEGER);
```

Here an attempt has been made to align the parameters of the procedure and to mark the first four parameters as inputs to the procedure and the last two as outputs. Even without an explicit English statement of the purpose of this procedure, there has been a gain in readability. The two one-word comments play a significant role in understanding. Using the words "inputs", "outputs", and "updates" (for parameters that are updated) is a simple convention that can be put to good use. We can do even better by using more descriptive (but still short) phrases, for instance,

```
procedure CHECKLINE ({using}    LINE:           STRING;
                                LINELENGTH:     INTEGER;
                     {look for}  STR:            STRING;
                                STRLENGTH:      INTEGER;
                     {giving}    var FOUND:      BOOLEAN;
                                var STARTPOS:   INTEGER);
```

Who needs much more comment than this?

If one takes an even more formal view, the full procedure header (code plus comments) should give a complete, almost technical specification of the unit. This view gives something like

```
procedure CHECKLINE ({using)    LINE:         STRING;
                                LINELENGTH:   INTEGER;
                     {look for}  STR:          STRING;
                                STRLENGTH:    INTEGER;
                     {giving)    var FOUND:    BOOLEAN;
                                var STARTPOS: INTEGER);
```

```
{ -- LINE has from 0 to MAXLINEWIDTH characters.
  -- STR has from 1 to MAXWORDSIZE characters.
  -- The search is for the leftmost occurrence.
  -- If not found, STARTPOS is given as 0. }
```

The preceding "marker" comments remind me of the cases where I have seen assertions used as comments. When used discretely they can be potent. For instance, the rather useless comments given earlier for a list of declared variables can be rendered:

```
var
   LINE: INPUTLINE;       { -- 0 through MAXLINEWIDTH characters }
   COL,                   { -- 1 through MAXLINEWIDTH}
   CURRENTCOL: POSITION;  { -- always >= COL }
   LEFTINDENT: INTEGER;   { -- 0 through MAXINDENT }
```

Other fine marker comments are:

```
while CONTINUESEARCH do { -- NUMDIFFS = 0 }
   ...
end;
```

and

```
else if EOLN (INFILE) then  { -- missing comma }
   begin
      ...
   end
```

Comments with Content

When it comes to annotating a procedure header, always take care to say only useful things. Sometimes a single line of text will do, other times a little more explanation may be needed. Consider the following:

```
procedure CHECK  ({for}   F: FILENAME;
                  {in}    var D: DIRECTORY;
                  {giving} var STATUS: FILESTATUS);
```

```
{ -- This procedure interrogates a directory D for the status of
  -- a file named F. The status returned is either
  --    NOTFOUND  if F is not in D
  --    CLOSED    if F is inactive
  --    OPEN      if F is open but not in use
  --    BUSY      if F is open but in use
  --    LOCKED    if F has been locked for restricted access }
```

Here the listing of status values returned by the procedure is substantive. I am not suggesting that such an itemization is always useful; perhaps the procedure body itself is so clear that itemizing particular status values is quite overbearing. But if that is not the case, the comment is helpful.

One difficulty is the need to restructure the code in cases where comments are otherwise needed. If a fragment of code needs a comment, perhaps the code itself could be improved. Consider the following example:

```
{ -- Insert entry into linked list }
GETCURRENTPOS(OLDPOS, NEWEL, LIST);
NEWEL↑.LINKPTR   := OLDPOS↑.LINKPTR;
OLDPOS↑.LINKPTR := NEWEL
```

There is no question that this comment is useful. Nevertheless, we do not have to accept the given code as is. Consider the following rendering of the preceding lines.

```
HITENTRY := FINDPOSITION(NEWENTRY, LIST);
NEWENTRY↑.LINK := HITENTRY↑.LINK;
HITENTRY↑.LINK := NEWENTRY
```

Here an attempt has been made to make the meaning of the code itself clearer. The original comment is less useful now. This brings up the general point that the way to avoid comments is to write code that speaks for itself.

Some comments tend to drag on and on. Such comments are often found at the beginning of a program or subprogram. As I mentioned earlier, the beginning of a program is often a wise place to put many comments. This is the major bridge from the problem to the program. These introductory comments can, in part, replace the need for external program documentation. External documentation is difficult to maintain and frequently fades into the background as time goes on. Putting the key documentation at the head of the program is one way to encourage the keeping of such documentation and to have the documentation where it is needed, in the program. Nevertheless, any idea can be implemented well or badly, and such is certainly the case for introductory program comments.

Let us look at Figure 4.1. We presume here that we are building a rather elaborate program to perform arithmetic operations on fractions. Such a program is far from trivial and may occupy many pages. It deserves some introductory explanation.

Figure 4.1   *Dribbling Comments*

```
program FRACTIONS (INPUT, OUTPUT);

{ --    This program performs arithmetic on fractions. All fractions are
  -- computed to the lowest common denominator. It prints results in
  -- fractional form. A fraction is denoted by a positive integer without
  -- a sign, followed by a slash, and another positive unsigned integer.
  -- These fractions can be combined in general arithmetic expressions
  -- using the conventional operators. As is the normal convention,
  -- multiplication and division take precedence over addition and
  -- subtraction.
  --
  --    The program uses several key variables in performing its
  -- computation. The first is CURRENTVAL. This variable holds the current
  -- value computed for the expression. Intermediate values are stored on
  -- a stack named STACKOFVALS. This stack is maintained during the course
  -- of the computation, and a pointer to its current depth (STACKPTR)
  -- specifies the number of items currently in the stack. The maximum
  -- stack depth is 100 entries. During the course of the computation, a
  -- number of errors can arise. These include expressions that are not
  -- well-formed arithmetic expressions, the use of symbolic names in
  -- expressions (which are not allowed), and the use of numbers with
  -- decimal points.
  --
  --    The main program calls three procedures. The first is GETINPUTEXP.
  -- This procedure gets the next expression from the user of the program.
  -- It handles the interaction with the user. The second procedure is
  -- PROCESSEXP. This procedure takes the string of characters given as
  -- input and evaluates it according to the normal rules of fractional
  -- arithmetic. The third procedure, called PRINTRESULT, prints the
  -- result of the computation. Each of the various procedures can result
  -- in the reporting of one or more errors.
  --
  --    The program can handle successive arithmetic expressions. These are
  -- input one at a time from the user as the user sees fit. When the user
  -- decides that enough expressions have been entered, the user can
  -- terminate the program once and for all by entering the word STOP in
  -- place of an expression. The entry of this word terminates the program.
  --
  --    The program begins with an introductory message to the user to
  -- enter expressions. Then the user enters an expression and the result
  -- is printed. All results are expressed as fractions. For example, the
  -- result THREE AND ONE-HALF is printed as 7/2. Errors in expressions
  -- input by the user are flagged as such, and the user must re-enter
  -- the entire expression according to the rules of the program. In
  -- these cases, a special message is given to the user. For example,
  -- the consecutive operators + - are not allowed. }
```

The facetious comments in the Basic program given earlier come to mind. The comments in Figure 4.1, however, might come from our assumed professional (P-sub-A). The comments require high mental concentration to read. There has been little attempt to separate out important points or to structure the comments so that they are meaningful. This brings up a side point about non-native English speakers. One hears the comment "I don't write English very well". This is usually an excuse for writing poor comments. One can get by with very little English and still make potent comments. The heart of the matter has to do with general presentation and thinking.

The comments in Figure 4.1 mention certain program details that are not important to the reader. The variables mentioned as well as the procedures called are hardly of interest. These comments are just as well left out.

The major problem with the example is a lack of discrimination. There is little attempt to structure the content, to list the exact conventions for well-formedness of expressions, or itemize the conditions leading to errors. The lack of examples is a persistent problem. Examples are great teachers, and they often make excellent comments. Nor is there any mention of major data structures, important algorithms, or the overall design.

Another crack at the introductory comments to our fractional arithmetic program is given in Figure 4.2. Here a different strategy is used. First, some key facts about the program, for example, its title and author are given. Then we have a brief summary, some examples, and then important technical details (only started in Figure 4.2). Although the comments of Figure 4.2 may not be the best (depending upon the actual program that is written), the comments are more useful than those of Figure 4.1.

An argument against the comments of Figure 4.2 is that they are, in part, really a summary of the user documentation. A user's manual must exist, so why be repetitious? Well, the programmer will indeed need the user manual for detailed coding. Nevertheless, the quick summary of Figure 4.2 is rich in content.

Comment Format

Everyone has a format for commenting, whether one realizes it or not. One of the most common formats is the following:

```
{ THIS COMMENT INTERFERES }
  PROCESSARRIVAL (DURATION);
  TIME := TIME + DURATION
```

This is one of the worst choices; the comment almost appears as part of the program itself. In Fortran or Basic where comments occupy an entire line, there is a tendency to line up all the comments with the lines of the program. In the preceding example, the "T" in "THIS" is aligned with the "P" in "PROCESS".

Figure 4.2   *Substantive Comments*

```
program FRACTIONS (INPUT, OUTPUT);

{ -- ** PROGRAM TITLE:  FRACTIONS
  --
  -- ** AUTHOR:  Cristie L. Jones
  -- ** DATE STARTED:  July 10, 1985
  -- ** DATE FINISHED: October 5, 1985
  --
  -- ** SUMMARY:
  --      This program takes as input lines of text, each presenting an
  -- arithmetic expression containing fractions. It computes the fractional
  -- result of each expression.
  --      The program terminates when a line is given beginning with the
  -- word STOP.
  --
  -- ** SAMPLE DIALOGUE:
  --      Computer:  PLEASE ENTER ONE OR MORE LINES EACH
  --                 REPRESENTING A FRACTIONAL EXPRESSION:
  --      User    :  1/8 + 1/8
  --      Computer:  1/4
  --      Computer:  NEXT EXPRESSION:
  --      User    :  1/4 + 1/3
  --      Computer:  7/12
  --      Computer:  NEXT EXPRESSION:
  --      User    :  ((3/32)*8
  --      Computer:  ** INVALID INPUT, TRY AGAIN:
  --      User    :  (1/8 + 1/2)*3 - (2/8)/(1/16)
  --      Computer:  -17/8
  --      Computer:  NEXT EXPRESSION:
  --      User    :  STOP
  --
  -- ** INPUT CONVENTIONS:
  --      (a) All values are given as whole, positive integers
  --      (b) The operators +, -, *, and / are allowed.
  --      (c) The operators * and / have precedence over + and -;
  --          otherwise evaluation is left to right.
  --      (d) Parentheses indicate grouping.
  --      (e) Consecutive operators are not allowed.
  --
  -- ** ERRONEOUS INPUTS:
  --      1/-2             needs 1/(-2)
  --      (1/8 + 1/2       needs closing parenthesis
  --      1/2 + +1/2       no successive operators
  --      A/2 + A/2        no symbolic names
  --      1/2 + 0/2        zero not allowed
  --
```

Figure 4.2 *continued*

```
-- ** MAJOR DATA STRUCTURES:
--    INBUFFER   the string of characters in an expression
--    STACK      a stack of components of an expression in postfix order.
--    ERRORNAME  an enumeration of the names of each input error.
--    FRAC       a record containing the numerator and denominator of a
--               fraction.
. . .              . . .
```

The problem is especially acute when the comment and the program text are both in upper-case or both in lower-case. The preceding excerpt, as well as the lines

```
{ So Does This One }
ProcessArrival (Duration);
Time := Time + Duration
```

share this fault. Shifting the comment over a bit, as in

```
{ Not Much Better }
ProcessArrival (Duration);
Time := Time + Duration
```

gives only a small improvement.

We can easily go to the other extreme and make the comments so strong that they assume a visual importance that is even greater than the program itself. For instance, consider the following:

```
{ ***** TOO STRONG ***** }
ProcessArrival (Duration);
Time := Time + Duration
```

Here the asterisks draw great attention to the comment when what counts are the two lines following the comment. The asterisk convention has even led a number of programmers to draw boxes around comments, for example,

```
{ * * * * * * * * * * * * * * * * * * * *
  *                                     *
  *            Boxes Get Ugly           *
  *       1. They overshadow the code.  *
  *       2. This is not Hollywood.     *
  *                                     *
  * * * * * * * * * * * * * * * * * * * * }
```

For some reason, this is assumed to be attractive. For me, it is the wrong direction. I have also seen the following convention:

```
                        { This stands out too much. }
    PROCESSARRIVAL (DURATION);
    TIME := TIME + DURATION
```

This kind of format gives the comments a littering effect and pushes the right margin of the program so far off that one might as well use the asterisks.

A better solution to the problem is to distinguish the comments from the program text in subtle ways. For instance, we might have

```
    { This is ok }
    PROCESSARRIVAL (DURATION);
    TIME := TIME + DURATION
```

Here lower-case is used for the comment and upper-case for the program text. My favorite convention is to embed an Ada-like comment (where all comments begin with two hyphens) into the text:

```
    { -- I like this }
    PROCESSARRIVAL (DURATION);
    TIME := TIME + DURATION
```

The double hyphen and its space give a nice three-character indent to the comment. The consistent use of the double hyphen also provides a gentle mark on each comment line. It makes it easy for the reader to scan the program for the comments or, on the other hand, to read the program and ignore the comments. A variant of this scheme, which uses lower-case for the comments as well as the program text, gives us something like:

```
    { -- I like this too }
    ProcessArrival (Duration)
    Time := Time + Duration
```

With the growing popularity of leading upper-case letters (as above) for identifiers, this convention seems a reasonable compromise, although my own preference is for a little more (but not too much more) discrimination.

Summary of Recommendations

Let me summarize my points about comments for high-level languages.

1. Use header comments.

2. Avoid in-line comments.

3. Use marker comments to describe procedure parameters.

4. Comment for content, not for dazzle.

5. Use a style that does not interfere with program reading.

6. Try to make the code say it all.

7. Be prepared to rewrite code that deserves a comment.

8. When in doubt, leave the comment out.

And, while we are here, when is the time to write a comment—*before* or *after* the code is written? In my mind, the answer is clear. The comment is less painful to write and will actually assist the author if done before the code.

Above all, remember, comments cannot turn a poor program into a good one.

5

One Procedure, One Purpose

Procedures are the basic unit for operational abstraction. They are the means by which a complex computation is packaged under a single name and isolated in the program text. The parameters define the inputs and outputs for the procedure, and the name of the procedure describes the intended computation. Here I wish to address a subtle problem that concerns the question: What is a suitable unit of computation? Put another way, When is the content of a procedure reasonable and when is it not?

Procedures should have a *single* purpose, a concept articulated in [Myers, 1978]. In the extreme, we would say that a procedure that updates a buffer, calculates a trajectory, prepares for the calculation of a new trajectory, and prompts the user for some input is hardly a single-purpose procedure. Imagine even trying to give such a procedure a meaningful name. But the issue of single purpose is subtle. There are many grey areas. I think that the right basis for evaluating the content is the problem domain itself. This means that implementation considerations, language considerations, and convenience are not appropriate. If we ask whether the procedure serves a single purpose in terms of the problem domain, we can hope for a better answer.

Initialization

Consider the procedure of Figure 5.1. This kind of procedure is familiar to almost every programmer. The purpose of this procedure is to initialize some items defined in a program. It has a simple name, INITIALIZE.

Many programmers would never question the procedure. We could argue about the use of global variables in this procedure, but its *purpose* is seldom questioned. Doing without the procedure of Figure 5.1 would necessitate some redesign of the program strategy. For one, some of the items initialized by this procedure would perhaps be initialized in the main program or the calling routines where these items are, in fact, updated as well. Some actions may need to be initialized in other procedures or packaged in a procedure of their own. Which technique is used depends on the *content* of the program itself.

So, what is the problem with the procedure of Figure 5.1? I submit the following:

1. Page numbers have little relation to buffers; the time and date have little relation to reverse video.

2. The other uses of the declared items will be scattered in various procedures throughout the program.

3. Not all of the initializations are likely to be needed at the beginning of execution.

4. Getting the initializations "over with" is hardly interesting.

Figure 5.1   *A Procedure with Many Purposes?*

```
procedure INITIALIZE;

    { -- This procedure initializes the files, print controls,
      -- buffers, and usage parameters for the on-line manual. }

var
    CODE: USERCODE;
    TIME, DATE: INTEGER

begin
    PAGENUM := 1;
    PARANUM := 1;
    LINENUM := 1;

    WINDOWSIZE := 10;
    MARKERCOL   := 1;
    REVERSEVIDEO := OFF;
    SIMULPRINT   := OFF;

    WORDPTR  := nil;
    SKIPWORD := EMPTY;

    for I := 1 to BUFFERSIZE do
        BUFFER[I] := BLANK;
    RESET(MANUALFILE);
    GETUSERCODE(CODE);
    LINKMANUAL(MANUALFILE, CODE);


    CLEARSCREEN(MANUALWINDOW);

    GETTIME(TIME);
    GETDATE(DATE);
    GETPROFILE(CODE, ASSUMPTIONS);
    SETUPUSER(ASSUMPTIONS, TIME, DATE);
    SETUPSCREEN;
end;
```

5. It is difficult to explain the purpose in specific terms.

6. The full parameter list (were we to have no global variables) is lengthy.

You see, this procedure certainly has a single purpose with respect to the program, but hardly a single purpose in the *problem* domain. In the problem-oriented domain, the purpose of the procedure is as follows:

1. Establish page and layout controls.
2. Establish initial screen controls.
3. Clear the input buffer and the current word entry.
4. Prepare the files containing the on-line user manuals.
5. Establish a screen for a new interactive session.

Note that calling five separate procedures *may* be a valid solution, but more likely a combined approach (as previously suggested) is the solution. We need to know the full problem.

Gray Areas

Procedures can assume their multipurpose nature in rather odd ways. One of the most common that I have encountered is a procedure that ostensibly has a single purpose, but if we look closely, it has some rather questionable supporting purposes. Here the line is often fuzzy. What is extraneous and what is intrinsic to the procedure? A careful sense of balance should prevail, and there are no clear-cut answers. Let us look at Figure 5.2.

Externally, this procedure seems to have a single purpose: that of deleting items from an ordered list. On many fronts, it is excellent.

The first questionable item comes into play when the list happens to be empty. No action is taken in such a case. One could argue that the empty list case should not be handled by the procedure, but rather by its caller, which should detect an empty list before the procedure is called. This matter seems subject for debate.

It may also happen that the list does not contain the item. This seems the normal for such a procedure, but the action taken by the procedure comes under some question. The procedure prints an error diagnostic. This brings up the difficult area of message reporting and whether it should be part of the procedure that detects the error or, rather, should be encapsulated into a single procedure. There seems no clear general solution to this matter and this issue falls into the grey area as well.

A third point, I believe, is not as questionable. The procedure reads in the item code of the item to be deleted. The reading of data from the user normally deserves a place of its own, where the proper format of the input can be checked and any oddities for error handling can be encapsulated in a single place. Putting this read action into the procedure DELETEITEM begins to muddle the real purpose of the procedure. Moreover, the procedure even prints a prompt for the next item to be deleted. This does not belong in the procedure.

Even if one were not to agree on these matters, there is a general problem with the procedure in that there is just too much going on. I do not wish to imply that there are procedures that are in fact quite complex, but the procedure given in Figure 5.2 exhibits complexity of behavior to the *caller*. The caller must be aware that

Figure 5.2   *Too Much Going On?*

```pascal
procedure DELETEITEM (var L: ITEMLIST);

    { -- This procedure reads in the identification code for an item
      -- to be deleted from an ordered list and deletes it. }

    var
        ITEM,
        PREVIOUSITEM: ↑ITEMINFO;
        VALUE: INTEGER;

begin
    if (L = nil) then
        WRITELN('*** Attempt to delete from an empty list.')
    else
        begin
            WRITELN ('Enter code for item to be deleted: ');
            READLN (VALUE);
            if (VALUE = L↑.CODE) then
                L := L↑.NEXT
            else
                begin
                    PREVIOUSITEM := L;
                    KEEPSEARCHING := TRUE;
                    while KEEPSEARCHING do begin
                        ITEM := PREVIOUSITEM↑.NEXT;
                        if (ITEM = nil) then
                            begin
                                KEEPSEARCHING := FALSE;
                                WRITELN ('Item not found.')
                            end
                        else if (ITEM↑.CODE = VALUE) then
                            begin
                                KEEPSEARCHING := FALSE;
                                PREVIOUSITEM↑.NEXT := ITEM↑.NEXT
                            end
                        else if (ITEM↑.CODE > VALUE) then
                            begin
                                KEEPSEARCHING := FALSE;
                                WRITELN ('Item not found.')
                            end
                        else
                            PREVIOUSITEM := ITEM
                    end
        end;
        WRITELN ('Type a space to delete another item.')
end;
```

1. The list may be empty.
2. The item may not be found in the list.
3. The item code is read in.
4. Messages may be printed by the procedure.
5. A prompt for another item is printed.

All of this hardly falls into the category of the meaning of the words "DELETEITEM"

A Clear-Cut Example

Another kind of anomaly that tends to give procedures a multipurpose nature is that of preparing for successive calls. We can get ahead on one call in order to prepare for cases that will arise in the next call. This kind of problem is exhibited in Figure 5.3.

This procedure performs some simple organization of an array, presumably representing a deck of cards. We assume that the array initially has 52 entries, one for each card in a conventional deck. After certain playing operations, cards are removed, creating "holes" in the deck. The reorganization procedure removes any existing holes and compresses the array so that the remaining cards are at the beginning of the array. The procedure updates the running count of cards.

For example, consider the following array:

```
A:  C3 D10 _ _ S7 S12 _ D1 _ C11 D4 _

NUMINDECK: 12
```

Here 12 items are to be examined. When the holes are removed and the existing cards are pushed to the beginning of the array, the result is the following:

```
A:  C3 D10 S7 S12 D1 C11 D4 _ _ _ _ _

NUMINDECK: 7
```

For this procedure a number of types are assumed. These are as follows:

```
type
   CARDINDEX  = 0..52;
   SUITLETTER = (C, D, H, S, NONE);
   RANKNUMBER = 1..13;
   CARDINFO   = record
                   SUIT: SUITLETTER;
                   RANK: RANKNUMBER
                end;
   DECKINFO   = array [CARDINDEX] of CARDINFO;
```

Figure 5.3   *A Procedure to Reorganize an Array*

```
procedure REORGANIZE(var DECK: DECKINFO; var DECKSIZE: CARDINDEX);

   { -- This procedure updates an array DECK of cards so that empty positions
     -- are eliminated. DECKSIZE gives the index of the last position to be
     -- examined. For instance, with
     --
     --       A: C3 D10 _ _ S7 S12 _ D1 _ C11 D4 _
     --
     -- we have as output
     --
     --       A: C3 D10 S7 S12 D1 C11 D4 _ _ _ _ _
     --
     -- If the array is empty, a new array with a full 52-card deck is created.
     -- If the array is initially full, an error diagnostic is printed. }

   var
      RANKVALUE: RANKNUMBER;
      SUITVAL:   SUITLETTER;
      I, COUNT:  CARDINDEX;

begin
   COUNT := 0;
   for I := 1 to DECKSIZE do begin
      if (DECK[I].SUIT = NONE) then
         { do nothing }
      else
         begin
            COUNT        := COUNT + 1;
            DECK[COUNT] := DECK[I]
         end
   end;

   if (COUNT = 0) then
      begin
         for SUITVALUE := C to S do
            for RANKVALUE := 1 to 13 do begin
               COUNT := COUNT + 1;
               DECK[COUNT].SUIT := SUITVALUE;
               DECK[COUNT].RANK := RANKVALUE
            end
         COUNT := 52
      end
   else if (COUNT = 52) then
      WRITELN ('Attempt to reorganize a full deck.')
   else
      DECKSIZE := COUNT
end;
```

A slightly dangerous thing is done with the type SUITLETTER in that the suits (clubs, diamonds, hearts, and spades) are represented in the enumeration type by a single letter. Printing suit names by their initial letter on the screen is a convenient pictorial form, but using single letters to represent these suits in a program is questionable. Nonetheless, our interest centers on the purpose of the procedure of Figure 5.3.

The primary purpose of the procedure is to reorganize the array. This part is fine. But now notice some other things that affect the behavior of the procedure.

1. If the deck of cards is initially empty, a new full deck is created. This seems inconsistent with the stated purpose. In this case, a better behavior would be to do nothing or, if need be, report back a status flag.

2. If the deck is initially full, an error message is printed. This hardly seems an error as far as the procedure is concerned and would be better detected elsewhere.

Item 1 is a case of preparing for the future. Such behavior has little business in the procedure.

The moral of each of the preceding examples is the same. A procedure should have one purpose. Purpose is defined with respect to the *problem* domain by its behavior to the *caller*.

6

Program Layout

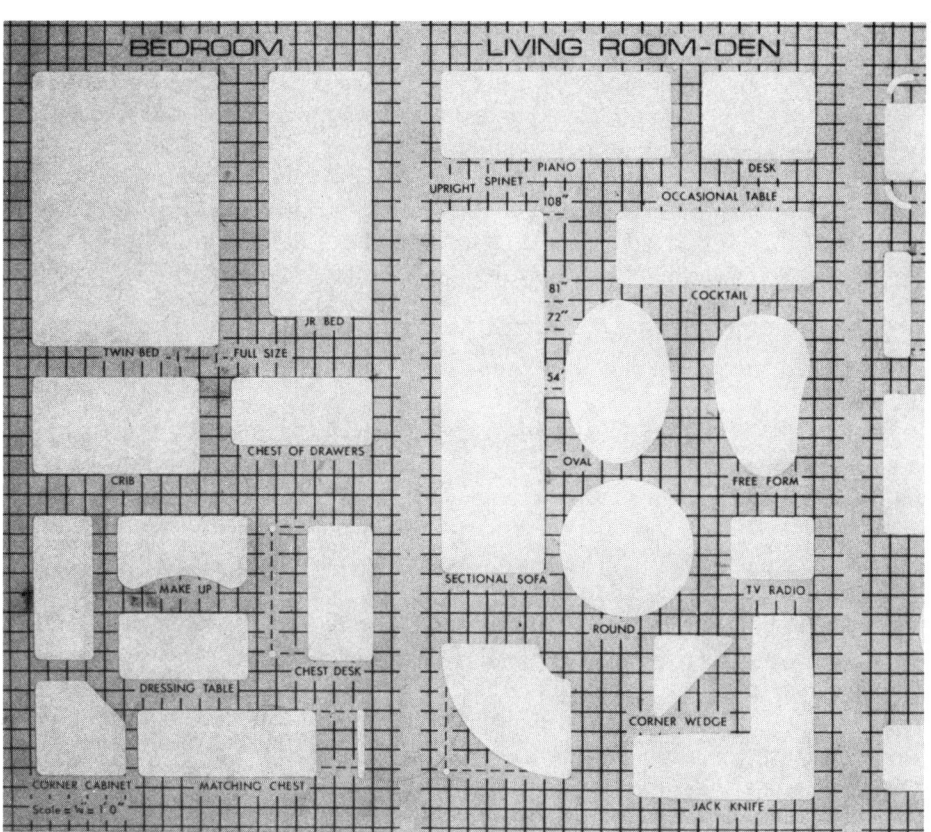

> Nothing more happened on the passage worthy of mentioning; so after a fine run, we arrived safely in Nantucket. (Herman Melville, *Moby Dick,* Ch. 14)

This was Ishmael's diary, but well may have been a remark made by the Captain in the ship's log, perhaps not much different from the many that we have read from the romantic days of tall ships and robust sailing.

Today, both sea and air navigators use logs to make remarks about the conditions of the environment in which they are sailing or flying. But the log is also a guide to document where they have been and where they are going. Once the coded symbols are understood, anyone familiar with the language should be able to pick up a completed log and reconstruct the trip or the mission without undue difficulty.

Table 6.1 is an abbreviated format of a log that a professional navigator would prefer. For the sake of brevity, some items such as altitude, true air speed, and outside air temperature are not listed; but the form itself, even in this brief format, will serve the purpose of our discussion.

This is a fairly standard layout for a professional aerial navigator's log. It is logical in that not only are data recorded of what happened, but that data can be used to project what will happen next. For example, halfway between leveling off at altitude and Point A, he made a simple observation of the compass reading and the clear air turbulence. When our airborne Magellan reached point A, he discovered that he arrived earlier than he predicted—ergo, the groundspeed that he experienced was 20 knots higher than he predicted. To project his arrival time at Point B, he will use this updated information to establish another ETA. Were a like log recovered from an airliner that had crashed, anyone familiar with the codes would be able to reconstruct the flight path for several hours before the incident.

In most aerial operations in the Air Force today, especially in the Strategic Air Command (SAC), these kinds of logs become a matter of record. Not only do line navigators keep these logs, but they are reviewed by the professional staff navigators. I have a friend who served in this capacity for a number of years and he told me many stories of how he was, after an onerously long time, able to reconstruct a mission of a young navigator only with difficulty. Here is the case of the professional examining the product of a journeyman P-sub-A. Ours is not the only profession in which there are degrees of competence functioning in the profession. The difference may be that the Air Force has put some checks and balances into their system with the long-range goal of continually upgrading the P-sub-A to professional. Oh, I wish... .

With a P-sub-A log, all the information is there—true. But? Although the professional reader can find the information needed to reconstruct the mission, he has to go from one section of the log to another. The information is not consistently recorded in a logical format. One is always having to look for something, even though it is there.

Three degrees of expertise have been demonstrated: the novice or the amateur who makes the simple observation that the trip to Nantucket was

Table 6.1 *A Navigator's Log*

TIME	TC	W/V	DR	TH	VAR	MD	DT	GS	TIME	TG	ETA	REMARKS
1900	090	360/15	-5	085	-15	070	—	250	:07	30	1907	CLIMB-OUT
1907							30	250				LEVEL OFF
1907	045	330/45	-7	038	-15	023	—	470	:45	350	1952	TO Pt. A
1925						023						WX: TURB
1950							350	490	:43			OVER Pt. B.

Key:

TC	=	True Course	GS	=	Ground Speed
W/V	=	Wind Direction and Velocity	DT	=	Distance Traveled
DR	=	Drift Correction Angle	TG	=	Distance to Go
TH	=	True Heading	ETA	=	Estimated Time of Arrival
VAR	=	Magnetic Variation	WX	=	Weather Observation
MH	=	Magnetic (compass) Heading	TURB	=	Turbulence

pleasant; the P-sub-A navigator who, perhaps, not a fault of his own making, fills out a haphazard log that although it contains the necessary information, is difficult to read; and the professional who selects the proper format and manages it professionally.

Rationale

Many computer programs are designed with much attention to overall organization, but I cannot understand why this organization is not clearly displayed in the program's format. For example, most everyone indents the body of a for loop and inserts some blank lines and page breaks and that is about it.

Let me define what I mean by program layout, or "pretty-printing" as it is sometimes called. This is the use of blank lines, blank spaces, page breaks, and alignment within a program. The purpose is not window dressing, but a *visible* display of *meaning*.

Like our three observing navigators, here are three cases of programmers doing what they do according to their level of competence, in this instance: amateur, P-sub-A, and professional. Behold the amateur:

```
READ(NUM);
if (NUM>0)and(NUM<MAX)
then SUM := SUM+NUM else
WRITE('Out of Range')
```

I must confess that when I originally used this as an example, I had a credible computer engineer edit this short portion of a program and he came up with:

```
READ (NUM);
if (NUM > 0) and (NUM < MAX) then SUM := SUM + NUM
   else WRITE ('Out of Range')
```

We could debate this layout, and, for some readers, this is what the professional writes:

```
READ (NUM);
if (NUM > 0) and (NUM < MAX) then
   SUM := SUM + NUM
else
   WRITE ('Out of Range')
```

I submit that the third alternative is superior to the others. In these cases, I am accused of arguing for nothing but symmetry, but oh, what a difference. I think that most programmers would attempt to make the small effort to clarify such simple statements if only they thought about symmetry. But there is much more to the issue than illustrated by this simple comparison—the issue is deeper and much more far reaching.

Over the years as an author and teacher, I have reviewed at least 50 textbooks on programming. From all of those that are either out of print or *au courant,* I can only think of a handful whose program layout I would consider better than mediocre; I can think of no better identification tag for a P-sub-A programmer than most of the programs displayed in textbooks that purport to teach or enlighten the field of computer science. Those who write texts for instructional purposes surely know that their programs are to be read by the ignorant, the novice, or the amateur. Readability, especially the lower down the scale one goes, is absolutely paramount. Yet most of the time, readers must struggle with inconsistencies in program layout that are strictly due to the author's lack of attention.

Why is program layout important? It would be an insignificant issue if programs were never read by people, and this is the point: programmers too often are only concerned that a program "works." The author should be concerned that *others* will read the program.

Of course the author reads the program—many times over. He or she reads it many times while it is being entered, edited, and revised. It has to be read carefully when test cases are generated, when bugs are being located, and when the program is generally checked over. It would be hard to quantify the amount of times an author reads his own program, but I would think that he spends twenty to fifty times more time in reading the program than in typing it.

As for larger projects and program maintenance, the norm for professional software, demands for precision and readability are even greater. People other than the author have to interact with (i.e., read) the program under varying circumstances and conditions. Readability, once the program leaves the author's jurisdiction, is a dominant attribute of a properly produced program. The later reader will be able to judge in a moment how much attention the author gave to program layout.

Carefully thinking about program layout may actually drive the design and writing of the program itself, as the program develops an aesthetic of its own. Good program layout follows systematically from a clear understanding of the program. In my experience, few lines of code exist that cannot be improved by proper attention to layout. Everything from module structure, program headers, comment sections, and expressions must be considered.

Consider the following sequence of statements:

```
WRITELN(NumDollars:2,' Dollars');
WRITELN(NumHalfs:2,' Halves');
WRITELN(NumQuarters:2,' Quarters');
WRITELN(NumDimes;2,' Dimes');
WRITELN(NumNickels:2,' Nickels');
WRITELN(NumCents:2,' Cents');
```

In this case, the program fragment is not very complicated and doesn't even do very much. It simply prints some values with a notation of what the values stand for. Most programmers I have met would not give the layout a second thought.

On closer inspection, we can make a few observations. First, the code is sandwiched and condensed. This is symptomatic of the blur of code that is often found in larger fragments. Second, we notice certain meanings in the program fragment. The most obvious are that each call to WRITELN has two parameters, and on each call the arguments have the same role: a value and an annotation. As a minor matter, each value is printed with a field width of 2. Furthermore, each quoted string annotating the values begins with a space. All these points will have to be proofread at some point. Now examine a professional rendering of the same computation:

```
WRITELN (NumDollars :2, ' Dollars' );
WRITELN (NumHalfs   :2, ' Halves'  );
WRITELN (NumQuarters:2, ' Quarters');
WRITELN (NumDimes   ;2, ' Dimes'   );
WRITELN (NumNickels :2, ' Nickels' );
WRITELN (NumCents   :2, ' Cents'   );
```

The code now speaks for itself. Even the error is easier to detect.

A Lurking Principle

Consider the following expression:

```
A + B * C
```

In most languages multiplication is performed before addition. As a result, B is multiplied by C and the result is added to A. This gives rise to the following alternative layout, a conventional one adopted by many programmers:

```
A + B*C
```

This rendering is superior in that the reader does not have to remember the precedence of multiplication over addition. The matter is clear just from the printing. In the extreme, no one would print the preceding expression as

```
A+B * C
```

The reason here is obvious—the layout has completely the wrong suggestion. All of this is traditional, but there is a principle lurking behind this simple matter. This principle is: *Program layout can be used to display conceptual units.*

Consider also the following simple assignment:

```
Z:=A
```

Here there is no space around the assignment operator, and, although I would prefer the space, the need is not urgent. But next consider the following:

```
Z:=A + B*C
```

Here the lack of space around the assignment operator is quite distracting. Reading the assignment as written suggests that A is assigned to Z and then something else is done to add the results of the multiplication. This simple statement, of course, is better rendered as

```
Z := A + B*C
```

Logically the important point of this construct is that it has a left side (a variable) and a right side (an expression). The expression itself has two constituent parts, namely, the operands of the addition. To be absolutely clear about these matters, we could write the statement as

```
Z := (A + B*C)
```

or

```
Z   :=   A + B*C
```

Both alternatives make the hierarchical nature of this statement even more visible. They are, however, unpleasant to the eye. In the larger context of assignments with longer variable names, they can become quite obtrusive. Herein lies the matter of taste. It is easy to go too far with program layout. Good program layout requires balance and sensitivity. The principle, though, is the same—*the visual display of conceptual units.*

At a slightly higher level, consider the following fragment:

```
COMPAREMORE := TRUE;
RESET (PRINTFILE);
LINENUM := 1;
ASSIGN (FILEA, 'PREVRESULTS');
ASSIGN (FILEB, 'NEWDATA');
while COMPAREMORE do begin
   COMPARELINES (LINENUM, LINESTATUS)
   if LINESTATUS = DIFFERENT then
      begin
         COUNTDIFFS (LINENUM, NUMDIFFS);
         ...
end;
```

This fragment performs some comparison of two files. Such a fragment typically occupies 30 or 40 lines. The game here is to identify conceptual units. In this fragment the first few lines perform some initializations, and the loop performs a major calculation on two files. The separate roles of the two parts can be clarified with a blank line, as in

```
ASSIGN (FILEA, 'PREVRESULTS');
ASSIGN (FILEB, 'NEWDATA');
RESET (PRINTFILE);
CLEARBUFFER;
LINENUM := 1;
COMPAREMORE := TRUE;
while COMPAREMORE do begin
   COMPARELINES (LINENUM, LINESTATUS)
   if LINESTATUS = DIFFERENT then
      begin
         COUNTDIFFS (LINENUM, NUMDIFFS);
         ...
end;
```

Notice here the liberty in rearranging the initialization statements. This brings up a little programming quirk: leaving an unnecessary distance between the initialization of a variable and the body of code where it is updated.

▬▬▬*Reflecting Everyday Presentation*

The preceding examples typify *program* logic. There is another fairly elementary principle that is almost universally violated. Wherever applicable, *guidelines for good conventional presentation should govern the layout of programs.*

To start with, there is a simple everyday rule of English usage that a space appears after a comma. The space is a mark of separation. For instance, few would write prose like

apples,oranges,bananas

or

x,x+1,x-1

Yet programmers seem to insist on writing things like

```
var
    NUMAPPLES,NUMORANGES,NUMBANANAS: INTEGER;
```

or

```
WRITE(X,X+1,X-1)
```

The difficulty here is that, when no space follows the commas, the items that are separated tend to become cluttered, sometimes almost impossible to decipher. For example, lines like

```
WRITE('Values are',X:4,', ',X+1:4,', ',X-1:4)
```

are more clearly written as

```
WRITE ('Values are', X:4, ', ', X+1:4, ', ', X-1:4).
```

Even this is still not easy on the reader, and perhaps something like

```
WRITE ('Values are', X      : 4,
       ', ',          X + 1 : 4,
       ', ',          X - 1 : 4);
```

is better. The goal is to show meaning, not to force readers to scrutinize punctuation.

I have also been mystified by what I call the "floating colon". Consider the following:

```
var
    LINENUM, PAGENUM : INTEGER;
```

The funny thing about this little fragment is that one's eyes almost immediately go to the colon. The fact that the colon is necessary is purely a grammatical point, hardly of interest to the program reader. Something like:

```
var
    LINENUM, PAGENUM: INTEGER;
```

appears preferable.

A common violation of good presentation appears in the comment sections of programs. Admittedly most programmers do not particularly enjoy writing comments. They are not much fun and they are really there for the use of other readers, not the author. Nevertheless, comments can be useful, especially when they appear at the head of a module and describe its overall function.

If you are going to write a comment, especially a long comment describing the purpose of a significant computation, you should take special care. As an elementary starter, follow normal English paragraphing conventions, for example, begin each paragraph with an indent of several spaces and separate paragraphs by blank lines. Even the conventional filling of the lines to achieve a not-too-ragged right edge can be important; when not done, the comments have a littering effect. When it comes to indented items such as an equation or a list of names, these items should be block indented from the main text and separated from the body of text by blank lines. For instance, rather than

```
{ - This procedure returns the roots
  - of the equation A*X+Y + B*X + C. If A is zero, ...
```

use

```
{ - This procedure returns the roots of the equation
        A*X+Y + B*X + C
  - If A is zero, ...
```

Even this simple guideline is violated over and over again.

Comb Structures

I would next like to discuss an issue that was first drawn to my attention during the development of Ada [see Chapter 2, Ada Rationale, 1979]. This is the use of "comb-like" structures as a method of program layout. A comb structure is just what the name implies, a structure that has the shape of a comb:

The comb structure is an alternative to the "toothbrush" structure:

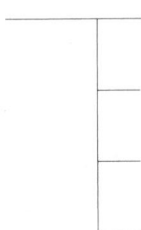

Both have a place, but the differences are noteworthy.

Consider the following type declarations:

```
type OPTION = (DIRECTORY, EDIT,     SEARCH,
               PRINT,     GENERAL, TEST,
               LIBRARY,   SAVE,     RUN);

     SYMBOL = record
                 NAME:   OPTION;
                 VALUE:  STRING;
                 LENGTH: INTEGER
              end;

     TABLEENTRY = record
                     CHOICE:   SYMBOL;
                     ARGUMENT: STRING;
                     OVERRIDE: BOOLEAN
                  end;

     KEY = packed array[1..MAXLEN] of CHAR;
```

The record structures here are combs, but the outer type declarations are toothbrushs. The first little problem here is that the text starts to drift across the page. Lining things up becomes a bit difficult. These problems are relaxed by using the comb structure.

```
type
   OPTION =
      (DIRECTORY, EDIT,    SEARCH,
       PRINT,     GENERAL, TEST,
       LIBRARY,   SAVE,    RUN);

   SYMBOL =
      record
        NAME:   OPTION;
        VALUE:  STRING;
        LENGTH: INTEGER
      end;
```

```
TABLEENTRY =
   record
      CHOICE:   SYMBOL;
      ARGUMENT: STRING;
      OVERRIDE: BOOLEAN
   end;
KEY = packed array[1..MAXLEN] of TABLEENTRY;
```

The comb structure rule here is: start each major unit on a new indented line.

Nested structures bring home the point even more clearly. Consider the following type declaration:

```
type TABLEENTRY = record
                     CHOICE: record
                                NAME:   (DIRECTORY, EDIT, SEARCH, PRINT,
                                         GENERAL, TEST, LIBRARY, SAVE, RUN);
                                VALUE:  STRING;
                                LENGTH: INTEGER
                             end;
                     ARGUMENT: STRING;
                     OVERRIDE: BOOLEAN
                  end;
```

Here we see the tendency of the program text to collide with the right margin. Rendering this with the comb structure, we have:

```
type TABLEENTRY =
   record
      CHOICE:
         record
            NAME:   (DIRECTORY, EDIT, SEARCH,  PRINT,
                     SAVE, RUN, TEST, LIBRARY, GENERAL);
            LENGTH: INTEGER;
            VALUE:  STRING;
         end;
      ARGUMENT: STRING;
      OVERRIDE: BOOLEAN
   end;
```

Here the collision is less severe, even in cases where the record structure is more complex than the simple example above.

The choice between comb and toothbrush is not always easy. Consider the following scenario:

```
while not EOF(INFILE) do
   begin
      GETCHAR (NEXTCHAR);
      if not IGNORECHAR (NEXTCHAR) then
```

```
            case NEXTCHAR.NAME of
                LETTER:   GETIDENTIFIER (INFILE, NEXTCHAR, NEWCHAR,
                            NAME, VALUE);
                DIGIT:    GETNUMBER (INFILE, NEXTCHAR, NEWCHAR, NAME,
                            VALUE);
                EOLNMARK: SKIPCHAR (INFILE);
                OTHERCHAR: begin
                            GETSPECIALCHAR (INFILE, NEXTCHAR, NEWCHAR,
                                NAME, VALUE);
                            ...
                         end
            end {case}
        end;
```

Here the toothbrush layout of the case alternatives is troublesome. Case statements, especially when nested within loops or conditional statements, have a tendency to lose their clarity. The text begins to collide with the right margin and lineup becomes difficult.

Now consider a pure comb-like rendering of the preceding example:

```
while not EOF(INFILE) do begin
    GETCHAR (NEXTCHAR);
    if not IGNORECHAR(NEXTCHAR) then

        case NEXTCHAR.NAME of
            LETTER:
                GETIDENTIFIER (INFILE, NEXTCHAR, NEWCHAR, NAME, VALUE);
            DIGIT:
                GETNUMBER (INFILE, NEXTCHAR, NEWCHAR, NAME, VALUE);
            EOLNMARK:
                SKIPCHAR (INFILE);
            OTHERCHAR:
                begin
                    GETSPECIALCHAR (INFILE, NEXTCHAR, NEWCHAR, NAME, VALUE);
                    ...
                end
        end {case}
end;
```

Here the clash with the right margin is eased. On the other hand, we could argue here that the case labels are not quite as visible as in the previous version.

The comb structure inspires my preference for the printing of program units (procedures, functions, and modules). For instance, in

```
procedure
    -- declarations
begin
    -- statements
end;
```

the comb structure is provided by the keywords **procedure, begin,** and **end.** The comb structure also inspires my preference for the layout of loops with compound bodies as

```
while (A < B) do begin
    -- statements.
end;

for V := 1 to 10 do begin
    -- statements
end;
```

This kind of alternative prevents the slight toothbrush effect as well as the deeper indentation required for forms like

```
while (A < B) do
    begin
        -- statements
    end;
```

Unfortunately, Pascal if statements do not readily allow the same convenient placement of **begin** and **end** symbols and so more strained solutions must be employed.

Layout Rules

To some degree, but *only* some degree, program layout conventions can be written down as specific rules and even automated. Table 6.2 lists some conventions that I recommend. Once in a while I have shown conventions like these to a class and discussed the reasons why I believe such conventions to be useful. By the end of the discussion, usually after some minor debate and changes, there is universal agreement that such conventions should be followed. The surprise comes weeks later when, in the heat of the moment, the conventions fall by the wayside. This does not undermine my belief that such conventions are sound and should be followed to the very last detail.

One of the best solutions for fixing the rules is to automate them. The spread of automatic program editors, which sometimes do far more than layout, can be a great blessing. When well designed, such editors can relieve the tedium faced by the careful craftsman.

There is a small feature that I have never seen automated. Write a five-line comment paragraph, neatly formatted. Now make a change, say delete a word or add a sentence. What happens? All the neatness gets ruffled. You may have to alter every line to get back a neat prose appearance. The layout system could be told that the paragraphs are comments and rejustified automatically. In the absence of this feature, it is understandable why comments often slowly degrade.

Table 6.2   *Some Program Layout Conventions*

1.   The **begin** and **end** symbols of a program, function, or procedure should start at the left margin. This prevents the difficult situation of trying to indent contained procedures, for example, trying to write:

```
program MAIN(INPUT, OUTPUT);
    ...
    procedure PROC1;
        ...
        begin
            ...
        end;
    ...
end.
```

It is better to use page breaks (or 3 to 5 blank lines) to separate procedures and start them at the left margin. This will use extra paper, a tiny price.

2.   Let P and Q be two adjacent program units (e.g., a procedure, function, or module). The two units P and Q should be separated by a page break or at least 3 blank lines.

3.   Let P and Q be two adjacent program constructs (e.g., a case statement, for loop, sequence of assignments, or some program fragment with a single purpose). The two constants P and Q should be separated by at least one blank line.

4.   In constant, type, and variable sections, the introductory words **const**, **type**, and **var** should occupy separate lines. The relevant declarations should be displayed as a comb structure. Thus

```
const BLANK = ' ';
      LINELENGTH = 72;
type LETTER = 'A' .. 'Z';
     LINE = array[1..LINELENGTH] of CHAR;
```

would be better as

```
const
    BLANK = ' ';
    LINELENGTH = 72;

type
    LETTER = 'A' .. 'Z';
    LINE = array[1..LINELENGTH] of CHAR;
```

5.   Every statement should begin on a separate line. For example, avoid things like

```
LINECOUNT := 0;  PAGECOUNT := 0;
```

and write

Table 6.2 *continued*

```
LINECOUNT := 0;
PAGECOUNT := 0;
```

There are a few (but rare) exceptions, for example, initializing two parallel arrays.

6.   Each line of a program should fit comfortably on the width of a conventional 8-1/2 by 11 inch page. This means keeping all lines shorter than 72 characters (with 10 pitch print) or 80 characters (with the smaller 12 pitch print). Ordinary binders and copy machines will like this convention.

7.   While and for loops with compound bodies are displayed in comb form

```
while condition do begin
    -- statements
end;

for V := value-1 to value-2 do begin
    -- statements
end;
```

8.   If statements are displayed as

```
{ -- single choice }
if condition then
    statement

{ -- binary choice }
if condition then
    statement
else
    statement

{ -- 3-way choice }
if condition then
    statement
else if condition then
    statement
else
    statement
```

(Note: The Pascal *if* constructs resist good spacing.)

9.   While, repeat, for, if, case, and with statements can be nested. The total amount of nesting should not exceed five levels.

10.   The comparison operations (e.g., <, =, and >) and the assignment operator (:=) should be preceded and followed by at least one space.

11.   In compound conditions requiring two or more lines, the conjunctions **and** and **or** should appear at the beginning (not the end) of a line For example, instead of

▨ Table 6.2 *continued*

```
if (NAME in [PARAGRAPH,VERBATIM,NEWPAGE])and
   (LINE.LENGTH < MAXLENGTH) then
```

and

```
while ((X1 > 0.0) or (X2 > 0.0)) and MOREPOINTS and
      (GRIDSTATUS = ON) do
```

use something like

```
if (NAME in [PARAGRAPH, VERBATIM, NEWPAGE])
and (LINE.LENGTH < MAXLENGTH) then
```

and

```
while MOREPOINTS
and  (GRIDSTATUS = ON)
and  ( (X1 > 0.0) or (X2 > 0.0)) do
```

12. At least one space appears after every comma. This means not writing

```
var
    ONEVARIABLE,ANOTHER,YETANOTHER: INTEGER;
```

or

```
WRITE (THIS,THAT,THEOTHER)
```

but instead writing

```
var
    ONEVARIABLE, ANOTHER, YETANOTHER: INTEGER;
```

or

```
WRITE (THIS, THAT, THEOTHER)
```

. . . .

▨*Summary*

Any list of conventions, however well inspired, can only go so far. The same can be said for automatic formatting programs. Without trying to put percentages where they don't really belong, I guess that they can account for about a third of the job. The real challenge in program layout comes from the specific nature of the program at hand. The issue is to illuminate meaning, and meaning is intimately associated with the code that is actually written.

Generally speaking, the programmer has four options to promote good layout:

1. The page break
2. The blank line
3. The blank space
4. Alignment

The page break (or 3 to 5 blank lines) is the basic unit for separating program units. Program units are those larger sections of program text that generally occupy a page or two and that serve a single purpose. A unit might be a half page of comments describing the overall purpose of a module. It might be a one- or two-page summary of the key tables organized throughout the program and presented as a comment. Other units might be a rather long declarative section of constant names and their values, the declaration part of a rather lengthy procedure, and, of course, functions and procedures themselves. The page break (or vertical white space) is the means by which these major boundaries of program organization are expressed in a visible way.

The blank line is the basic unit by which individual constructs or individual groups of statements are highlighted to show their common purpose. It may mean simply splitting constant declarations from variable declarations or separating a major for loop from the statements required for input and output. The blank line serves the same purpose as the page break, only the units on which a blank line has an impact are smaller, typically five to ten lines.

The blank space is the means whereby the constituents of a single line of text are highlighted. Blank spaces can be used to separated the individual arguments in a procedure call or the separate conditions controlling a single conditional statement. In a sense the page break is the macro-unit, the blank line is the mini-unit, and the blank space is the micro-unit.

On top of these considerations is the matter of alignment. Alignment is the means by which things achieve a vertical organization. This is why the individual statements of a begin-end block are usually left aligned. Alignment can also be used in many other contexts, including the fields of a record structure or the individual constituents of a procedure call.

Most programmers give only token homage to the matter of program layout. Something is usually done to improve the situation from utter chaos, but often not too much. A typical example is the program of Figure 6.1. This short program shows some concern for making things clear. A better version is shown in Figure 6.2. This is what the professional writes.

Figure 6.1   *Mediocre Program Layout*

```
program PRINTDATE(INPUT,OUTPUT);
{This program reads in a date given in the form MMDDYY and prints
 it in the conventional form.
 For example, 022243 is printed as February 22, 1943.
 No input checking is performed,
 i.e., the user must enter a valid date.}

const BLANK = ' '; NUMMONTHS = 12:
   MAXNAMELENGTH = 9;
type
   MONTHNAME = packed array[1..MAXNAMELENGTH] of CHAR;
   NAMETABLE = array[1..NUMMONTHS] of MONTHNAME;
var M1,M2,D1,D2,Y1,Y2: CHAR;
   MONTHNUM,I: INTEGER:
   BLANKFOUND: BOOLEAN;
   NEXTCHAR: CHAR;
   PRINTNAME: MONTHNAME;
   PRINTVALUE: NAMETABLE;

procedure SETNAMES(var PRINTVALUE:NAMETABLE);
   {Set up table of month names.}
      begin
         PRINTVALUE[1]  := 'January  ';
         PRINTVALUE[2]  := 'February ';
         PRINTVALUE[3]  := 'March    ';
         PRINTVALUE[4]  := 'April    ';
         PRINTVALUE[5]  := 'May      ';
         PRINTVALUE[6]  := 'June     ';
         PRINTVALUE[7]  := 'July     ';
         PRINTVALUE[8]  := 'August   ';
         PRINTVALUE[9]  := 'September';
         PRINTVALUE[10] := 'October  ';
         PRINTVALUE[11] := 'November ';
         PRINTVALUE[12] := 'December '
      end;

   begin
      SETNAMES(PRINTVALUE);
      WRITELN('Enter a date in the form MMDDYY:');
      READLN(M1,M2,D1,D2,Y1,Y2);

      if M1 = '0' then
         begin
            if M2='1' then MONTHNUM:=1;
            if M2='2' then MONTHNUM:=2;
```

Figure 6.1   *continued*

```
            if M2='3' then MONTHNUM:=3;
            if M2='4' then MONTHNUM:=4;
            if M2='5' then MONTHNUM:=5;
            if M2='6' then MONTHNUM:=6;
            if M2='7' then MONTHNUM:=7;
            if M2='8' then MONTHNUM:=8;
            if M2='9' then MONTHNUM:=9
        end
    else
        begin {M1 = '1'}
            if M2='0' then MONTHNUM:=10;
            if M2='1' then MONTHNUM:=11;
            if M2='2' then MONTHNUM:=12
        end;
    PRINTNAME := PRINTVALUE[MONTHNUM];
    I := 0;
    BLANKFOUND := FALSE;
    while (not BLANKFOUND) and (I < MAXNAMELENGTH) do
        begin
            I := I + 1;
            NEXTCHAR  := PRINTNAME[I];
            if NEXTCHAR = BLANK then BLANKFOUND := TRUE
            else WRITE(NEXTCHAR);
        end;
    WRITELN(' ', D1,D2,', ','19',Y1,Y2)
end.
```

Figure 6.2   *Better Program Layout*

```
program PRINTDATE (INPUT, OUTPUT);

{  -- This program reads in a date given in the form MMDDYY
   -- and prints it in conventional form. For example,
   --     022243
   -- is printed as
   --     February 22, 1943
   -- No input checking is performed, i.e. the user must enter a
   -- valid date. }

   const
      BLANK  = ' ';
      NUMMONTHS = 12;
      MAXNAMELENGTH = 9;

   type
      MONTHNAME = packed array [1..MAXNAMELENGTH] of CHAR;
      NAMETABLE = array [1..NUMMONTHS] of MONTHNAME;

   var
      M1, M2,
      D1, D2,
      Y1, Y2,
      NEXTCHAR:   CHAR;
      BLANKFOUND: BOOLEAN;
      I, MONTHNUM: INTEGER;
      PRINTNAME:  MONTHNAME;
      PRINTVALUE: NAMETABLE;



procedure SETNAMES (var PRINTVALUE: NAMETABLE);
   { -- Set up table of month names. }
begin
   PRINTVALUE[1]  := 'January  ';
   PRINTVALUE[2]  := 'February ';
   PRINTVALUE[3]  := 'March    ';
   PRINTVALUE[4]  := 'April    ';
   PRINTVALUE[5]  := 'May      ';
   PRINTVALUE[6]  := 'June     ';
   PRINTVALUE[7]  := 'July     ';
   PRINTVALUE[8]  := 'August   ';
   PRINTVALUE[9]  := 'September';
   PRINTVALUE[10] := 'October  ';
   PRINTVALUE[11] := 'November ';
   PRINTVALUE[12] := 'December '
end;
```

Figure 6.2   *continued*

```
begin
   SETNAMES (PRINTVALUE);
   WRITELN ('Enter a date in the form MMDDYY:');
   READLN (M1, M2, D1, D2, Y1, Y2);

   if M1 = '0' then
      begin
         if M2 = '1' then MONTHNUM := 1;
         if M2 = '2' then MONTHNUM := 2;
         if M2 = '3' then MONTHNUM := 3;
         if M2 = '4' then MONTHNUM := 4;
         if M2 = '5' then MONTHNUM := 5;
         if M2 = '6' then MONTHNUM := 6;
         if M2 = '7' then MONTHNUM := 7;
         if M2 = '8' then MONTHNUM := 8;
         if M2 = '9' then MONTHNUM := 9
      end
   else
      begin { -- M1 = '1' }
         if M2 = '0' then MONTHNUM := 10;
         if M2 = '1' then MONTHNUM := 11;
         if M2 = '2' then MONTHNUM := 12
      end;
   PRINTNAME := PRINTVALUE[MONTHNUM];

   I := 0;
   BLANKFOUND := FALSE;
    while (not BLANKFOUND) and (I < MAXNAMELENGTH) do begin
      I := I + 1;
      NEXTCHAR := PRINTNAME[I];
      if NEXTCHAR = BLANK then
         BLANKFOUND := TRUE
      else
         WRITE (NEXTCHAR);
   end;

   WRITELN (' ', D1, D2, ', ', '19', Y1, Y2)
end.
```

7

A Purist's View of Structured Programming

It is hard to imagine a book about contemporary programming without a discussion of *structured programming*. The term structured programming has become a sort of modern buzzword. After all, who could be for "unstructured" programming, whatever that is? But then, for that matter, what is "structured" programming?

What Is It?

If I had never seen the term structured programming before, I would be hard pressed to give a definition of what the term might actually stand for. The word programming is obvious, it means the act of writing a computer program. But the word structured is more puzzling. A structure is some organization or some limit that we put on behavior. Thus structured programming could mean any one of many constraints: keeping all modules to a maximum length of one or two pages, the prohibition of nested procedures, restricted nesting of control structures to three or four levels, forbidding the use of global variables, or some such thing. As it turns out, the conventional definition of structured programming is tied exclusively to limits on the use of control structures.

As far as I know, the term structured programming was first used by Dijkstra in his monograph *Notes on Structured Programming* [see Dahl et al., 1972]. The term appears in the title, but not in the text. I believe the term was meant as programming (i.e., the process) in a systematic way, just what the words imply.

In any case, popular wisdom has it that *structured programming* is a method of programming with the following constraint: only one-in, one-out control structures are allowed. Traditionally these control structures are basic actions, if-then-else statements, and while loops. More generally, any of the control structures given in Figure 7.1 are allowed. All of these control structures have the property of being one-in, one-out.

The use of the term "one-in, one-out" begs a definition. In simple terms, a one-in, one-out control structure is any control structure that has precisely one entry point and precisely one exit point. We must be careful here. The definition implies that we cannot leave the control structure somewhere in the middle. The definition effectively rules out exit statements and goto statements. In these cases we would have a sequence of actions that could be prematurely terminated. This means, for instance, that if there are *n* basic actions in a while loop, then all *n* actions must be executed. It also means, for instance, that if a conditional statement is executed, control must always pass on completion of the conditional statement to the statement immediately following the conditional statement. In this way the conventional exit statements and goto are thus prohibited.

One could imagine other one-in, one-out control structures. An error-handling mechanism that caused the invocation of a special procedure when an error occurred and that resumed execution at the place where an error occurred would be one example. The important point is simply that the static structure of the program, as written on the page, always determines the sequence in which actions are taken. There can be no jumps to remote locations that abandon a given execution sequence.

The Two Guarantees of Structured Programming

Why is all of this important? Programs written with only one-in, one-out control structures have two dramatic advantages. First, the use of such control structures allows us to develop an almost static model of the flow of control within a program. The idea of flow of control almost disappears. For instance, when reading a while loop with no embedded exits or abrupt termination, we do not have to think of the idea of executing one statement, then executing another statement, and so on until control is passed back to the beginning of the loop. Instead we can think of the loop as simply a series of fixed actions that are executed as long as a particular condition is true.

Figure 7.1   *Some One-in, One-out Control Structures*

Basic Action: Assignment

```
X := X + 1
```

Basic Action: Procedure call

```
GETLINE (LINE, LENGTH)
```

Compound Action: Sequence

```
action-1;
action-2;
...
action-n;
```

Conditional: If-then statement

```
condition => action
```

Conditional: If-then-else statement

```
condition => action-1
else     => action-2
```

Conditional: Select-first

```
condition-1 => action-1
condition-2 => action-2
condition-3 => action-3
else        => action-4
```

Conditional: Select-case

```
case N of
  1      => action-1
  2, 4   => action-2
  3, 5   => action-3
  ...
  else   => action-n
end
```

Loop: While loop

```
while condition do
  actions
end
```

Loop: Repeat loop

```
repeat
  actions
until condition
```

Loop: For loop

```
for V := 1 to 10 do
  actions
end
```

Conditional statements follow the same line of thinking. We do not need to think of "jumping" to an action when a condition is true. Rather, we think simply that under certain conditions certain actions happen.

The second advantage of one-in, one-out control structures is that the conditions under which an action of a loop is taken or terminated are stated explicitly. Moreover, the relevant conditions are stated at the beginning or the end of the given construct. Thus we do not have to "look inside" for this information.

Consider the following

```
if (TABLEENTRY = NULLITEM) then
    . . .
    -- actions
    . . .
end
```

Here we imagine a lengthy sequence of actions that are only executed if a particular entry is null. Next consider the following fragment

```
while (COUNT < STORAGESIZE)
and (BUFFER[COUNT] <> STOPCODE) do
    . . .
    -- actions
    . . .
end
```

Here we know that whatever happens inside the loop upon termination control will continue following the end of the loop. We also know that upon termination one of two things will have happened, either the counter will indicate that storage has been exhausted, or a stop code has called for a halt to things. These facts are important. We do not have to search inside the loop to discover them. These then are the "guarantees" of structured programming:

- Control flow is always linear.
- Termination conditions are always explicit.

It has been my repeated experience that programmers who are used to other forms of control structures (especially those in assembler language) anguish about programming with the now traditional one-in, one-out control structures. Invariably, the older techniques, which allow exits and jumps, lead to a certain kind of thinking about programming. When these possibilities are removed, programming, at first, takes longer. It is not simply a matter of switching from one habit to another. The one-in, one-out structures force a discipline and an organization on our thinking process.

The Remaining Debate

Gotos and exits used to be a subject of more controversy than they are today. Nevertheless the arguments for them are much more refined and need to be dealt with. One argument goes like this.

> Forcing one to eliminate gotos and exits is unnatural. If I need to exit an algorithm and perform some wrapup activities, why should I be forbidden to do so? If I am careful, I can write perfectly clear programs with exits and even gotos. If all exits and gotos lead to a single point, the structure that arises is perfectly clear. The banning of these alternatives just restricts creativity and forces awkward solutions. Moreover, the wise use of labels and exits avoid artificial Boolean-valued variables. These variables obscure an otherwise clear piece of code.

The crux of the argument comes down to cases like this.

> So, what is wrong with the following code?

```
repeat
   GETDATA (INFILE, VALUE);
   if EOF(INFILE) then
       exit
   PROCESSDATA (VALUE)
until (VALUE = 99)
```

> Surely, the one-in, one-out alternative,

```
GETDATA (INFILE, VALUE);
while (not EOF(INFILE)) and (VALUE <> 999) do begin
   PROCESSDATA (VALUE)
   GETDATA (INFILE, VALUE)
end
```

> is longer and even, perhaps, less clear.

My reply is this. It is true that exits are easy to use. It is true that the repeat-loop-exit is readable. It is true that there are many cases like this. *But,* especially in non-toy programs, we lose the guarantee that we never have to look inside for the exit condition. Programmers can rely on this guarantee.

You see, we first have to be convinced of the superiority of the general principles mentioned earlier. That is, one-in, one-out structures guarantee that no control flow surprises will exist and that exit conditions are explicitly stated. These guarantees are certainly worth something to the program reader, let alone the person who is maintaining the program.

The argument about trading exits and labels for Boolean-valued variables just does not work out that way in practice. Of course, using only one-in, one-out structures does occasionally require the addition of a Boolean variable, but these variables in themselves can add clarity to a piece of code. It is certainly clearer to keep the guarantees and see something like

```
if not ITEMFOUND then
   -- actions
```

than to arrive at the same actions from some remote branching statement.

Let me sum it up this way. The game is not to convert exits or gotos into alternative forms, but to

- Start with the problem.
- Program as if exits and gotos do not exist.

Simpler solutions will result, and the guarantees will be kept.

8

Using Types

Types are a ubiquitous topic. There are broad questions like: What is a type? What is an "abstract data type?" What does it mean to "encapsulate" a type? How are these ideas relevant to the practicing programmer?

Types also have a more mundane setting, be it an array, a record, or an enumeration of values. It is this more ordinary level that I wish to address here. It is my contention that certain details are often glossed over by the practicing programmer. The result is a blurring of the fine concepts that even a simple Pascal-like facility for types can embody.

▉▉▉▉*Type Name vs. Variable Name*

A thorny problem arises in languages that allow programmers to define types. The dilemma is the choice between

- The name for a type.
- The name for a variable of the type.

Consider the following:

```
type
    TABLETYPE = array[1..10] of INTEGER;
var
    TABLE: TABLETYPE;
```

Here the convention used is to add the suffix TYPE to a type name and then to declare a variable with the same name, minus the suffix. A variant on this theme is the following:

```
type
    TABLEARRAY = array[1..10] of INTEGER:
var
    TABLE: TABLEARRAY;
```

Here the convention again is to add a suffix, a syntactic one, which identifies the type name as denoting array.

The preceding examples may seem innocuous, but I have seen hundreds of examples using these conventions, for instance,

```
LINETYPE        OPCODETYPE
COLORTYPE       CARDARRAY
HEADERTYPE      BOARDARRAY
```

The problem with these names is that they are purely syntactic. A better strategy is to think about what the type represents, and then to give the type a name that reflects its deeper meaning, for instance,

```
LINEINFO        OPCODEFORMAT
COLORNAME       DECKOFCARDS
HEADERSTR       BOARDSTATUS
```

But this is not all. Consider the declarations of Figure 8.1.

Figure 8.1 *Questionable Type and Variable Names*

```
{ -- 1. Personalized variable name }
type
   COLOR = (RED, WHITE, BLUE);
var
   MYCOLOR: COLOR;

{ -- 2. Specialized variable name }
type
   DAY = (MON, TUES, WED, THURS, FRI);
var
   DAY1, DAY2: DAY;

{ -- 3. Plural type name }
type
   MODES = (READONLY, WRITEONLY, READWRITE);
var
   COUNT: INTEGER;
   FILEMODE: MODES;

{ -- 4. Plural array type }
type
   ELEMENTS = array[1..10] of INTEGER;
var
   TABLE: ELEMENTS;

{ -- 5. Abbreviated variable name }
type
   COLUMN = 1..72;
var
   COL: COLUMN;

{ -- 6. Variable name suffix }
type
   ITEMTABLE: array[1..500] of ITEM
var
   ITEMARRAY: ITEMTABLE;
```

There are problems with each of the solutions in Figure 8.1.

1. Personalized names have little place in good professional practice. Reading

   ```
   if MYCOLOR = NEXTCOLOR(PLAYER) then ...
   ```

   is hardly illuminating.

2. Specialized names can work, but they can also be forced. DAY1 and DAY2 are only good if there are indeed two days at the same time.

3. A predefined type like INTEGER has a singular name. We speak of "the type integer". A type itself will have many members, but the name of the collection is singular. The inconsistency in using plurals can be seen in the declarations for COUNT and FILEMODE. COUNT is an INTEGER, but is FILEMODE a MODES? Type names should be singular.

4. Even plural array types look strange.

5. This is not bad, but the phrase

   ```
   COL: COLUMN;
   ```

   stumbles because the reader will read COL as COLUMN itself.

6. In my opinion, the use of syntactic variable names (e.g., ITEMARRAY or NODERECORD) is poor, giving situations like

   ```
   ITEMARRAY[I] := ITEMARRAY[J]
   ```

What to do? I offer these rough guidelines:

- The variable name (not the type name) deserves the priority. Variables occur much more often than type names. They also are the centerpiece of the code.

- The type should be named for what it really stands for. For instance, in a program RED is the *name* of a color, not a color.

- The variable should be named for what it really stands for, semantically.

- The algorithm (versus the declarations) should read well.

- *Meaning* is the game!

Although an ultimate naming choice depends markedly on the program as a whole, I would start with those in Figure 8.3. These may not be perfect, for naming is always hard. But I believe they are better.

Figure 8.3 *A Better Start*

```
1.  type
        COLORCHOICE = (RED, WHITE, BLUE);
    var
        COLOR: COLORCHOICE;

2.  type
        WEEKDAYNAME = (MON, TUES, WED, THURS, FRI);
    var
        HOLIDAY, NEXTHOLIDAY: WEEKDAYNAME;

3.  type
        MODESTATUS = (READONLY, WRITEONLY, READWRITE);
    var
        FILEMODE: MODESTATUS;

4.  type
        TABLE = array[1..40] of INTEGER;
    var
        SCORE: TABLE;

5.  type
        COLPOSITION = 1..72;
    var
        COL: COLPOSITION;

6.  type
        ITEMTABLE = array[1..500] of ITEMINFO;
    var
        ITEM: ITEMTABLE;
```

Unnamed Types

Consider the familiar declaration

```
A: array[1..10] of INTEGER;
```

The variable A is declared to have a given type, but the type is not named. Another unnamed type appears in the following:

```
R:  record
        X: REAL;
        Y: REAL;
        Z: REAL
    end
```

Consider also

```
type
   BOOKINFO = array[1..MAXNUMPAGES] of
                 record
                    NUMLINES: INTEGER;
                    HEADER:   HEADERINFO;
                    ARTWORK:  BOOLEAN
                 end;
```

Here we have a type named BOOKINFO, which is declared to be an array of records, but the record type itself is not named. This is also what I consider to be an example of an unnamed type.

The problem with unnamed types is that the type names should convey certain semantic information, even if used only for one variable. This example can be better rendered as

```
type
   PAGEINFO =
      record
         NUMLINES: INTEGER;
         HEADER:   HEADERINFO;
         ARTWORK:  BOOLEAN
      end;
   BOOKINFO = array[1..MAXNUMPAGES] of PAGEINFO;
```

Here we see a symmetry between PAGEINFO and BOOKINFO, and the types are introduced one at a time.

Consider the following:

```
type
   LINEMODE = (TEXT, EQUATION, TITLE);
   HEADERINFO =
      record
         POSITION: (LEFT, CENTER, RIGHT);
         CONTENT:  array[1..HEADERSIZE] of CHAR
      end;
var
   LINE,
   PREVLINE:   array[1..LINESIZE] of CHAR;
   LINESTATUS: LINEMODE;

   BOOKDATA:
      array[1..MAXNUMPAGES] of
         record
            NUMLINES: INTEGER;
            HEADER:   HEADERINFO;
            ARTWORK:  BOOLEAN
         end;
```

```
INFILE,
OUTFILE:  TEXT;
```

We can get by with declarations like this and many programmers adopt this style. In particular, some of the types declared for variables are given explicitly rather than named in a type declaration.

There are several problems with the preceding example. First, Pascal requires that procedure parameters be identified by type name, rather than by giving the definition of the type. This is a sensible rule, which guarantees that the type expected for an argument must be the same as that defined for the parameter. It means that we cannot say things like

```
procedure ILLEGAL (L: array[1..LINELENGTH] of CHAR);
```

We first must say something like

```
type
    LINE = array[1..LINELENGTH] of CHAR;
```

and then write

```
procedure NOWLEGAL (L: LINE);
```

This simple rule forces the programmer to name many of the types in a program.

But not all variables are passed as arguments to procedures and we often still get by with the example declarations given earlier. In fact there is a tendency to use such declarations just because it's shorter to give the type explicitly than to go to the trouble of giving it a name and its own type definition.

The example declarations show a certain inconsistency. Types like TEXT and LINEMODE are given by name, whereas the three arrays and a record structure are not. Most importantly, we must deduce exactly what these type definitions mean.

Next consider the following rendering of these declarations:

```
type
    LINEMODE      = (TEXT, EQUATION, HEADING);
    HEADERPOSITION = (LEFT, CENTER, RIGHT);

    LINETEXT   = array[1..LINESIZE] of CHAR;
    HEADERTEXT = array[1..HEADERSIZE] of CHAR;

    HEADERINFO =
        record
          POSITION: HEADERPOSITION;
          CONTENT:  HEADERTEXT
        end;
```

```
PAGEINFO =
   record
      NUMLINES: INTEGER;
      HEADER:   HEADERINFO;
      ARTWORK:  BOOLEAN
   end;

BOOKINFO = array[1..MAXNUMPAGES] of PAGEINFO;

var
   LINE,
   PREVLINE:   LINETEXT;
   LINESTATUS: LINEMODE;

   BOOKDATA: BOOKINFO;

   INFILE,
   OUTFILE: TEXT;
```

Here we follow a single convention: every type definition is given a type name identifying its purpose. This leads to simpler and clearer definitions. In passing, we also avoid the problem with procedures in that all parameter types will already be named.

Enumerated Types

Enumerated types are familiar to most programmers. They are conceptually simple and easy to use. The sins in this area are probably those of omission rather than commission.

The following simple example comes to mind

```
var
   FILESTATUS: BOOLEAN;
```

Here we have a variable that takes on one of two values. Boolean is a heavily used type in its own right, but it tends to be overworked. Instead, consider the following:

```
type
   FILEMODE = (ACTIVE, CLOSED);
var
   FILESTATUS: FILEMODE;
```

Here the type FILEMODE also has only two values. However, the advantage of this rendering is that its two values more closely convey the semantic information required for the variable FILESTATUS. There is no reason to shy away from enumeration types even when they have two values.

A simple generalization of this use comes with cases in which a variable has two "proper" values, but yet lurking in the program is the possibility that the values may be unknown and this itself is of interest. A simple recourse here is to add a third value to the proposed enumeration type. This value represents the idea of being "unknown", or "undetermined". For instance, consider

```
type
    RESPONSE = (YES, NO, UNDETERMINED);
```

Here the explicit possibility of the response being undetermined is treated up front, with a value of its own.

The idea of an unknown, unspecified, and undetermined value makes sense in many contexts. For instance, consider

```
type
    COMMANDNAME =
        (SINGLESPACE, DOUBLESPACE, PAGE, INDENT, HEADER, ERROR);
    ARGSTATUS =
        (VALID, INVALID, OUTOFRANGE, UNSPECIFIED);
```

Here both of these enumeration types have an additional value (the last one given). These values require special action on the part of the program.

Generally speaking, enumeration types can be used wherever a programmer needs to record the "state" of knowledge or to record that certain events have happened. One classic case is that of error conditions. For instance, we may have

```
type
    ERRORSTATUS =
        (MISSINGCOMMA, MISSINGARG, EXCESSCHARS, OUTOFRANGE);
```

Giving good mnemonic names to each error condition is useful in its own right. It also allows the value to be passed to procedures to take appropriate action or to issue diagnostic messages. In the line of extreme amateurism, I have seen something like

```
type
    ERROR =
        (ERROR1, ERROR2, ERROR3, ERROR4, ERROR5, ..., ERROR44);
```

This is a gross misuse of enumeration types. Here, rather than give each error condition a number, the programmer gives each error condition a numbered name. This is hardly an improvement.

Even messages themselves, not only for errors but for standard responses, often can be best captured by giving each message an enumerated name. For instance,

```
MSGNAME =
   (HELLOMSG,      BYEMSG,          PROMPTMSG,
    CONTINUEMSG,   MISSINGCOMMAMSG, MISSINGARGMSG,
    EXCESSCHARMSG, OUTOFRANGEMSG,   NULLMSG);
```

Here there is an explicit attempt to name each possible message generated by the program. Again, these values can be passed to procedures for the appropriate diagnostics. This simple strategy does not always work, for example, when messages have embedded parameters. However, in many cases it can have a profound effect by simplifying the handling of errors.

9

The Persistence of Global Variables

I now discuss what is surely a large and controversial issue—global variables.

It has been argued that global variables are one of the major culprits in programming. It is said that they destroy a program's logic, that they are dangerous, that they cripple program readability, and that they should be avoided altogether. Yet if you look at what people actually do with their own programs, it seems that almost no one pays any heed. Many amateurs, professionals, and textbooks either pay token homage to the idea or abandon it altogether. In elementary textbooks on programming, global variables abound.

Myers [Myers, 1978] gives the following arguments against global data:

- An apparent violation of structured programming principles.
- Unannounced changes to variables (side effects).
- Inability to use code in different contexts.
- Exposure of modules to more data than needed.
- Difficulty in managing access to data.

Dunsmore and Gannon [Dunsmore and Gannon, 1979] found clear performance difficulties as the number of "live" variables increased.

On the other side, some argue that the issue is highly overrated. It is said that globals can be wisely used, that they are not dangerous when handled well, and that, practically speaking, they are a necessity. Eliminating them is absurd.

Let us first clear up what a global variable is. To begin with we imagine a procedure P, which may or may not have its own local parameters (see Figure 9.1). The procedure will probably have some local declarations, for instance, constants, types, or variables. A variable is said to be *global* to a procedure if the variable is used within the procedure but not declared locally. Note here that constants and types, which may be declared globally, are not global *variables*. Also note that the definition is a relative one: a variable is global with respect to a given procedure. In Figure 9.1, for instance, we say that V is global to P.

Notice that the definition excludes variables that, even though they are globally "defined", are only used in procedures where they are mentioned in the parameter list. For instance, in

```
procedure COUNTBLANKS (var BUFFER: LINEINFO; var COUNT: INTEGER);
```

BUFFER may be defined globally but is not considered a global variable. Were the header changed to

```
procedure COUNTBLANKS (var COUNT: INTEGER);
```

then BUFFER would indeed be considered as a global variable.

In simple terms, if you have to look outside a procedure for the declaration of a variable, the variable is global. Later in this section we will consider "own" variables or "hidden" variables and their impact on the global variable issue. For the moment, though, let us talk about the conventional case, variables that have a use both within a procedure and outside it.

Figure 9.1 *A Global Variable V*

```
program GLOBALVAR (INPUT, OUTPUT);
   ...
   procedure P (var X,Y: INTEGER);
      local declarations
   begin
      ...
      X := V;  { -- V is declared at outer level. }
      ...
   end;

begin
   ...
   V := V + 1;
   ...
end.
```

On Mental Abstraction

When we look at statements in a program, we always ask: What happens? What does it mean? We may have to struggle, but we search for its meaning. For instance, if we read

```
if BOARD[SQ] = PLAYERSPIECE then
    begin
        if LEFTSQ <> NULLSQ then
            if BOARD[LEFTSQ] = VACANT then
                PATHFOUND := TRUE;
        if RIGHTSQ <> NULLSQ then
            if BOARD[RIGHTSQ] = VACANT then
                PATHFOUND := TRUE
    end;
```

we try to summarize the code in simple terms so that we may "read on". Informally, this code means

> Test if there is a legal path starting from square SQ.

But this is not really enough. A better abstraction is:

> Given
> - The status of BOARD
> - A square SQ

Update PATHFOUND to true if
- There is a free path to the left, or
- There is a free path to the right. ·

When we understand the code, we conceptualize it in terms of three variables: BOARD, SQ, and PATHFOUND. Our simple mental model is

```
BOARD, SQ -> PATHFOUND
```

If the code were the body of a procedure (or function), there would thus be two conceptual inputs and one output.

Let us look at the example given in Figure 9.2. This is a procedure assumed to be in a rather lengthy program that might be used for automatic testing of programs. The procedure tests if a line of the actual output is identical to the expected output.

On initial reading this procedure looks quite acceptable. The procedure has a single parameter, the line number of the two lines being compared for equality. The procedure has several local variables and performs some useful function. But now we have to ask: What does this program *really* do? Since this procedure obviously interacts with other portions of the program, we need to know its exact effect. This leads to a number of detailed questions:

1. Are the lines altered by the procedure?

2. Is the line position after the call available to the caller?

3. Are the tested lines being simply scanned, or are the line files altered by a call to the procedure?

4. Does the procedure send any control information back to its caller?

5. Are two successive calls to the procedure identical in effect to a single call?

The problem here is that we must look *inside* the procedure for the answers because the procedure does contain global variables. In particular, two external files are referenced in the procedure as well as a flag that is used outside the procedure.

These matters are not trivial. For one, it is possible to alter the external effect of the procedure from within. A caller must know that the external files are altered by the reading of a single line. No programmer can change this behavior without disrupting the program around it. It is also possible to cause problems from outside. For instance, we cannot change the name LINEFLAG elsewhere without undermining the integrity of the procedure. Both of these seemingly innocent issues tie this procedure to the rest of the program. The damage here is that this linkage is implicit.

Figure 9.2 *A Procedure with Global Variables*

```
procedure LINETEST (LINENUM: INTEGER);

{ -- Read a line from each of two files. If the lines are identical, set a
  -- flag to indicate the result. If the lines are not identical, the lines
  -- are printed with a marker under the first pair of differing characters. }

    var
        END1, END2,
        POSITION,
        LASTPOSITION: INTEGER;

        LINE1, LINE2: LINEIMAGE;
        CONTINUETEST: BOOLEAN;

begin
    GETLINE (FILE1, LINE1);
    GETLINE (FILE2, LINE2);
    END1 := LENGTH(LINE1);
    END2 := LENGTH(LINE2);
    if END1 < END2 then
        LASTPOSITION := END1
    else
        LASTPOSITION := END2;

    POSITION := 1;
    CONTINUETEST := TRUE;
    while CONTINUETEST do begin
        if POSITION > LASTPOSITION then
            begin
                LINEFLAG := SAME;
                CONTINUETEST := FALSE
            end
        else if LINE1[POSITION] <> LINE2[POSITION] then
            begin
                LINEFLAG := DIFFERENT;
                CONTINUETEST := FALSE
            end
        else
            POSITION := POSITION + 1
    end;
    if END1 <> END2 then
        LINEFLAG := DIFFERENT;

    if LINEFLAG = DIFFERENT then
        PRINTPAIR(LINENUM, POSITION, LINE1, LINE2)
end;
```

The general issue is again one of mental "abstraction". We tend to believe in the sanctity of simple assignments like

```
Z := F(X,Y)
```

This familiar line conjures up an implicit understanding that F has *only* two inputs, X and Y, and *only* returns a single value Z. We assume no side effects to global variables or implicit references to variables outside the function. Given values for X and Y, the value Z computed will always be the same, no matter what the context. This is a major reason for functions or procedures—to make the overall behavior of a program unit explicit.

If we were guaranteed beforehand that all the interactions in a procedure were explicitly listed in the header of the procedure, we could make our mental abstractions more quickly and know exactly what we can and cannot alter. The complete header for the procedure LINETEST should read something like

```
procedure LINETEST ({inputs}  LINENUM: INTEGER,
                    {updates} var FILE1, FILE2: TESTDATA;
                    {outputs} var LINEFLAG:    LINESTATUS);
```

This does not fully guarantee that there will be no surprises for the programmer, but at least makes it perfectly clear what the inputs and outputs of the procedure are as well as which items are updated in the course of the call. Now the procedure body can be altered at will as long as the parameters are held to their required behavior. From the outside as well, the procedure is then insulated from spurious connections through other parts of the code.

We might argue that the preceding revised procedure header indicates some problems. And it does. This is precisely a reason for listing all inputs and outputs in the first place. A better rendering of the procedure as a whole might be

```
procedure LINETEST ({inputs}  LINE1, LINE2: LINEIMAGE;
                    {outputs} var LINEFLAG: LINESTATUS);
```

Now the need for global variables disappears. Even better, the procedure might be cast as a function and the printing handled by the caller, for instance

```
function MISMATCH (LINE1, LINE2: LINEIMAGE): INTEGER;
{ -- Returns 0 if LINE1 and LINE2 are identical, and
  -- otherwise the position of the first mismatch. }
```

You see, the point here is a full awareness of the procedure as a "black box", with explicit inputs and outputs. Ultimately the programmer or reader *must* make this abstraction. Making the code say it as well exposes the real complexity of the black box.

The Case Deepens

We might ask why programmers persist in using global variables even though the case against them is generally understood and supported. One reason is "seduction". At first glance, it is a delight to see the sequence

```
GETDATA;
PROCESSDATA;
PRINTDATA;
```

This is, if you will, the classic program. It looks so simple. Yet if we ever have to read, modify, or maintain such a program, we must of course look at the procedures themselves.

Then come the hard questions: What data are being read? Are the data in a file? If so, which file? Are things like line numbers and page numbers printed with the data? Are there headings? Is there a particular format for the input data or the output data? Are there any buffers in which the data are stored internally? To have any rational degree of control over this program, such questions are paramount. With such a simple sequence, it is likely that some of the answers require quite a bit of global information, including global variables. The interactions on these variables are likely to spread across the pages of many procedure boundaries.

In the extreme, the result can be chaos. I have seen cases like

```
procedure EVENTLOG;
{ This procedure records and controls entries into the log. }

   var STATUSNEXT: EVENTREC;

begin
   LOGENTRY := 0;
   CLEARSCREEN;
   MSGAREA := FIELDA;
   DISPLAYBOX(32);
   NEWAREA := FIELDB
   LOG.COUNT := 0;
   LOG.STATUS := PREVSTAT;
   LOG.MSG := BLANKMSG;
   while STATUSCOND = CONT do
   begin
      FILLBOX(MSGAREA, DIAGCOUNT, NEWEVENT, EVENTSTATE,
              ITEM, RESULT);
      PROCESSEVENT(NEWEVENT, LOG.STATUS, RTNMSG);
      UPDATELOG(LOG, LOGENTRY, DIAGCOUNT, EVENTSTATE,
              NEWAREA, NEWDIAG, STATUSNEXT);
```

```
      if LOG.STATUS = CLOSED then
         if (LOG.COUNT > 0)
         and (NEWAREA = FIELDC)
         and (STATUSCOND = CONT) then
            LOGENTRY := 99
      else
         SETCONDITION(STATUSNEXT, EVENTSTATE)
   end;
   WRITEBOX('EVENT LOG', 10, 7)
end;
```

Everything is global. The mental management of code like this is virtually impossible.

But let us not dwell on the extreme. A common argument for global variables runs like this:

> Global variables can add clarity. If you pick out the global variables and list them in the procedure header, you haven't changed anything except that all the procedure calls will be much longer. It's worse to have procedures with long parameter lists than to put only the key variables in the parameter list. Variables that cross many procedure boundaries (for example, state information or a common data structure) should be left alone. Why add such complexity to the program at large?

One problem with the argument is that it is a "conversion" argument. The implicit assumption here is that we write a procedure with free use of all the variables in the program. The procedure header becomes simply a synopsis of what was actually used.

But this is precisely the wrong way to think about procedures. We should always write the interface for a procedure, that is, the procedure header, first. This should itemize exactly what the *complete* effect of the procedure is. In doing so we would spot a long list of parameters *before* the procedure was written. If the list became too long, it would be a signal that the design of the program itself was wrong.

In practice, if we design a program by spelling out the interfaces first, it is likely that the program itself will be reconceived to contain simpler and clearer interfaces. I have known a few, but all too few, programmers who avoid global variables completely. The long list of parameters that we expect from the conversion argument simply doesn't occur.

The conversion argument against global variables is just like the conversion argument that used to be given against avoiding goto's. Once upon a time people argued that getting rid of goto's would just result in a profusion of Boolean flags just to avoid a few simple labels. If we program without goto's in the first place, a different structure of the program actually arises, and the problem about the profusion of Boolean variables simply fades away. In practice there are usually very few.

I still have not really answered why programmers persist in using global variables. My best guess is that it requires great discipline, especially at first. Programmers must

- At all times think carefully about inputs and outputs.
- Write interfaces first.
- Be ready to reconsider an approach that becomes unwieldy.

Ultimately,

- Control the flow of data in exceedingly careful ways.

When the discipline is adopted, the results are usually far superior.

Own Variables and Information Hiding

The concept of *own* variables originally came from Algol 60. Here a procedure could declare a local variable that retained its current value from one call to another. The own variable could only be used in the procedure itself.

Common examples of own variables include the following scenarios:

1. Suppose we write a utility routine called READITEM for reading items from some external file. Conceptually, such a procedure has two parameters: the name of the file and the variable that will hold the next item to be read. For practical reasons it may be necessary to read groups of items into a buffer or storage area. For instance, it may be much faster to use a buffer, or it may be necessary to store a group of items in some intermediate form. In either case, the internal buffer holds items that are as yet unread by the caller. The variable denoting the buffer can be classified as an own variable.

2. Suppose we were writing a module to insert items into a data structure and to retrieve them later. From the caller's point of view there might be two visible procedures: a procedure PUTITEM to post items into the data structure and FETCHITEM to retrieve items from the structure. Such procedures would have one or more parameters reflecting the behavior as seen by the caller. But in writing such procedure it may be necessary to use a linked list structure with pointers to achieve the desired effect. These internal pointers and structures are entirely a matter private to the procedures themselves, of no concern to the caller. Such pointer variables can be classified as own variables.

3. Suppose we were writing a program to format text and control the printing of pages. The program might control indentation, paragraphing scheme, and headers. We could imagine a single procedure PRINTBLOCK

that takes a block of text and prints it in the required format. Subsequent calls to the procedure may add other blocks of text until an entire document is formed. Suppose further that page numbers are not under the control of the caller but are handled entirely by the procedure. A variable that, say, keeps track of the current page number after successive calls to the procedure would be an example of an own variable.

The point of these examples is one of information hiding. To perform some computation it may be necessary to hide certain information from the caller. This information is necessary to do the job of the procedure but immaterial to the caller.

Some contemporary languages do not have a special linguistic facility for handling these hidden variables. Such a facility is available in Ada with its idea of "packages", but not in Pascal. In Pascal, to write such procedures we must declare the own variables as global. See Figure 9.3. Own variables are not global variables in the sense mentioned earlier, since they are of no relevance to the caller. It is unfortunate, however, that in Pascal, a variable that is conceptually own must be declared globally.

Since own variables must be declared globally, there is the question of determining whether a globally declared variable is own or not. Put another way, if we restrict the use of global variables to those that are own, how can we tell whether a particular variable fits the definition of an own variable?

The test is one of usage. Suppose we are looking at a globally declared variable V. Suppose that procedure P is the *only* procedure to make use of or update V (apart from setting its initial value). Then V is own.

For variables that are shared by several procedures performing related actions, for example, the procedures PUTITEM and FETCHITEM, the same kind of reasoning applies. If V is *only* used within PUTITEM or FETCHITEM, then V is own.

I must say that I have some reservations about any discussion of own variables or information hiding. I do not want to "let the cat out of the bag" or provide a loophole in my basic point. Own variables have a limited scope. The crucial test is

- Is V known, used, or updated by the caller?

If so, the variable is *not* own.

In the three cases itemized earlier, we could change the scenario slightly and lose the own status.

1. If the caller needs to inspect the buffer, the buffer is not own.

2. If the caller accesses the pointers to free storage, the pointers are not own.

Figure **9.3** *An Own Variable*

```
program OWNVAR (INPUT, OUTPUT);

    ...
    -- declaration of V
    ...
    procedure USEOWN (parameters);
        -- This is the only procedure to use V
        -- (except for setting its initial value)
        ...
    begin
        ...
        V := V + 1;
        ...
    end;

begin { -- main program }
    V := 0;
    ...
end.
```

3. If the caller makes any use of page numbers (for instance, if the program user can ask to start numbering at page 10), the page number variable is not own.

It is a tight situation.

Summary

In summary, I would like to put it this way. Programs should not contain any global variables (except for those variables that must be declared globally in order to implement the concept of own). The reasons for prohibiting global variables are as follows:

1. To promote *better* program design.
2. To specify the *complete* role of a procedure.
3. To avoid reading *inside* a procedure to understand its external behavior.

It takes great discipline, but the rewards are greater.

10

The Difficulties with Nesting

The idea of nesting has been a part of programming for many years. The idea came into common parlance with the introduction of Algol 60. Since then the idea has been adopted in many languages now in popular use. These include Algol 68, PL/I, Pascal, Modula-2, and Ada.

The basic idea is that local definitions can be introduced into a program. A name can be identified with a meaning and the association between the name and its meaning extends only over a limited portion of the program text. The idea is most familiar in procedures. In particular, a definition introduced within a procedure applies only within that procedure. For instance, we may have

```
procedure P (parameters);
    I: INTEGER;
begin
    -- body of P
    -- local use of I
end;
```

Here the variable I is introduced and plays some internal role. The declaration of I does not apply outside P. Thus the name can be used freely outside the procedure with an entirely new meaning.

Aspects of Nesting

The value of allowing names to have local meanings is immensely useful to the practicing programmer. It allows the idea of procedure to assume its role as a "black box". As long as the interface specified through the procedure parameters is kept, any other internal workings of the procedure are hidden from outside.

In a typical case, a procedure will have an itemized list of parameters as well as local declarations. For instance, we may have something like

```
GETARGUMENT ({from}      LINE: LINEINFO;
             {updating}   var POSITION: COLNUM;
             {giving}     var ARGUMENT: INTEGER);
    const
        SPACE = ' ';
    var
        NEXTCHAR: CHAR;
        NEWPOSITION: INTEGER;
begin
    . . .
    -- body of procedure
    . . .
end;
```

Note here that the names of the parameters (LINE, POSITION, and ARGUMENT) as well as the declared constants and variables (SPACE, NEXTCHAR, and

NEWPOSITION) are local to the given procedure. These names may be used freely outside the procedure without regard to their specific meaning within GETARGUMENT.

A number of factors that influence the effectiveness or use of nesting include the following:

1. *Nesting of procedures within procedures.* In most block-structured languages, a procedure can itself contain a local declaration of another procedure. For instance, if procedure B is used only in procedure A, then B may be declared within A and the use of B is protected from outside.

2. *Nested blocks.* In some languages (not Pascal) a new scope of names can be introduced directly within a statement itself. This usually takes the form of a compound statement with local declarations. This use, although not at all as popular as nested procedures, allows the same kind of local protection of names.

3. *Packages.* With the growing popularity of packages or modules, these program units can also introduce a local name space. In Ada, for example, a package is a program unit that contains both a visible part (the names that can be exported to other program units) and a hidden part (the names of locally declared types, variables, and procedures) that is entirely protected from the outside.

4. *Separate compilation.* In a language that allows separate compilation of program units, there is usually a clear wall of protection of names. Just as in a library package of mathematical subroutines where the details are entirely hidden from the user, so too can the programmer make use of separately compiled program units to make a clear wall around the name space of a program unit.

5. *Global declarations.* The ability to hide names within nested program units usually comes with the ability to declare certain entities as global. A constant, type, variable, or procedure declared at an outer level may be used within any nested units (that is, until a new declaration of the same name appears). With the use of global items, the name space protection is only partial.

Issues like these tend to influence the way the programmer thinks about nesting and the protection of names.

Nested Procedures

Consider the following scenario, in which we have a main program that calls one declared procedure named A. The procedure A, in turn, calls one procedure named B; B, in turn, calls another procedure named C. In short,

```
MAIN calls A,
A calls B,
B calls C.
```

In this case only the procedure A need be made visible to the main program and B itself can be declared within A. Likewise, C is only called from B, and C itself can be declared within B. A display of such a program is given in Figure 10.1. This form is used by many programmers.

An alternative rendering of the same program is given in Figure 10.2. Here the procedures B and C are not nested. C is declared before B and both are declared before A. This is what I call the linear model of program organization. This organization, I suggest, is superior on several grounds.

The first thing to notice about the nested version in Figure 10.1 is the rather awkward layout required for the display of the program itself. In particular, the body of procedure A must be given after the bodies of both procedures B and C.

Figure 10.1   *Use of Nesting*

```
program MAIN;
    -- declarations for main program
    A: procedure;
        -- local declarations for A

        B: procedure;
            -- local declarations for B

            C: procedure;
                -- local declarations for C
            begin
                -- body of C
            end C;

        begin
            -- body of B
            -- calls C
        end B;

    begin
        -- body of A
        -- calls B
    end A;

begin
    -- main program
    -- calls A
end;
```

This interrupts the normal top-down reading sequence, which is to read

1. The body of A first.
2. The body of B second.
3. The body of C third.

Moreover, in a program of any size, the body of A itself may be pages away from its header declaration and the declaration of its local items. This forces considerable page flipping on the part of the programmer. It also brings up another issue. When reading the body of the procedure, what are its local declarations? These kinds of problems are entirely avoided by the linear display of Figure 10.2.

The nested organization of Figure 10.1 also begs the question: How important is it to provide protection for the names of procedures? Although protection of variables is certainly important, procedure names are far fewer in number than variable names. Moreover, procedures are in some sense like constants. We do not usually update a procedure to take on a new meaning. It is the variables that count as far as the dynamics of the program is concerned, and the procedures may be thought of as fixed, large, constant objects. Making the names of the procedures themselves global (a consequence of Figure 10.2, the linear display) hardly seems a burden.

The basic argument against the use of nested procedures is simply that it seems too extreme just to prove the point that a procedure is in spirit local to another procedure. The alternative linear rendering of Figure 10.2 provides a simple model for the programmer to grasp and a simple display of the program on the screen. The simplicity seems to outweigh the slight gains in protection.

There are a couple of minor difficulties with the proposal of Figure 10.2. It may be the case that a procedure like B introduces some local constants and types, which, in turn, are used by procedure C. In this case, the constants and types have to be declared at an outer level, in the main program itself. This exposes the types and constant names to a greater region of text than need be. The same argument can be posed for variables that are local to B but global to C. The global variable issue itself is a tricky one and my strong urging is to avoid global variables altogether. So, on the debit side, the problem seems to lie in the declaration of constant objects.

I would argue that exposing the names of constant objects to a greater region of program text than need be is not particularly damaging. The very nature of these kinds of objects, that they are constant, poses little mental overhead. Moreover, their occurrence is not as frequent as one might imagine. In practice, when a collection of procedures is grouped together, presumably for some common purpose, types and constants tend to be shared among several procedures. They then have to be declared at an outer level anyway.

Figure 10.2   *Linear Display*

```
program MAIN;
    -- declarations for main program

    C: procedure;
        -- local declarations for C
    begin
        -- body of C
    end C;

    B: procedure;
        -- local declarations for B
    begin
        -- body of B
        -- calls C
    end B;

    A: procedure;
        -- local declarations
    begin
        -- body of A
        -- calls B
    end A;

begin
    -- main program
    -- calls A
end;
```

11

It Worked Right the Third Time

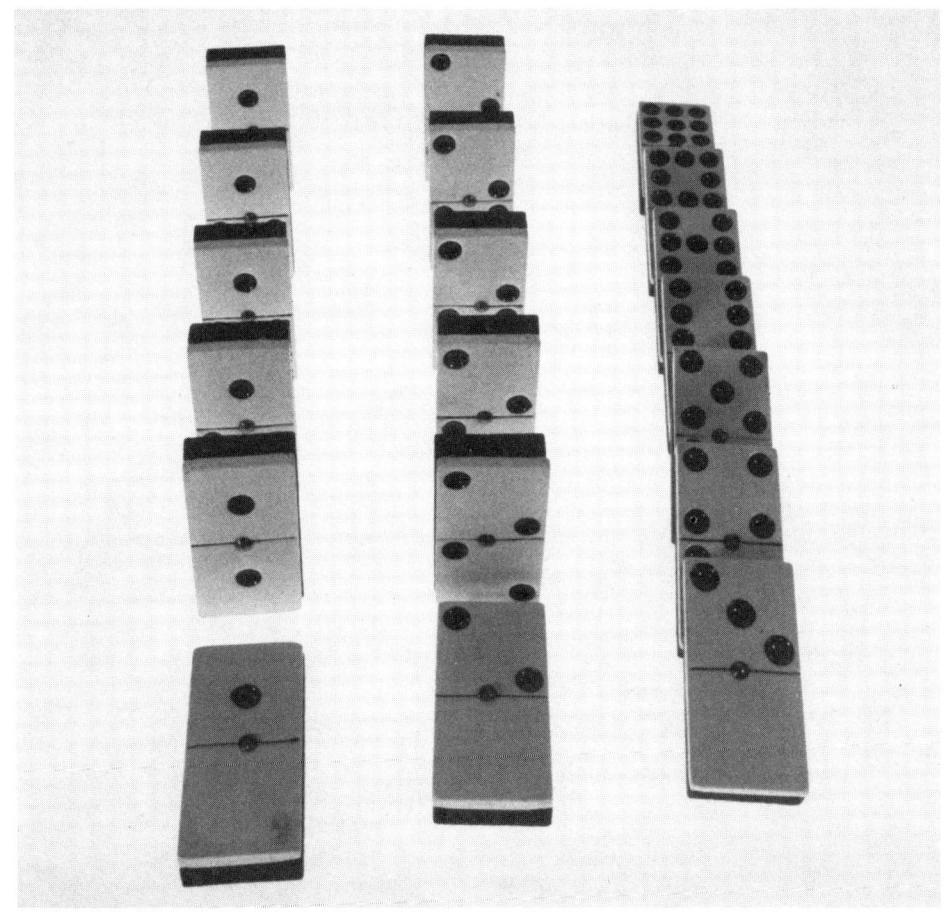

The British, who revere golf as a distinct part of life, have a term for a stratum of golfers that lies beneath the amateur and pervades the game in such a way that the members of this class may dominate the game more than any "superstar" could wish. They comprise the majority of golfers who were the substance of a survey in the United States which reported that the average score across the country was 108. They are the "coarse" golfers. Any knowledgeable golfer can identify them by simply watching them go off the first tee of a municipal golf course any warm Saturday morning in June.

The coarse golfer has a poor memory and may report his score for any one hole as anything between 8 and 13. He is seldom seen on the fairway, some have been reported as missing persons as they disappear into the heavy undergrowth where most of their game is played. But when the coarse golfer reaches the green, he has one abiding goal: lay your fourth putt dead. Although he seldom succeeds, he keeps trying to get it right—and sometimes he does.

In any sport, of course, no one ever gets it right the first time every time. But if precision is unobtainable where it is not expected, it can be obtained where it *is* expected. In the professional world of software programming, we elevate our sights above "coarse" programming, but too often we are satisfied not that we got it right the first time, or the third time, but the ninety-third time. Why should this be?

A Fairy Tale

Here is a contrived example:

> Recently appointed as vice president in charge of technical management of the Partco Corporation, a large international distributor of foreign auto parts, you receive your first assignment for the upcoming year: to purchase a comprehensive inventory and billing software for your company.
>
> Computer expertise within the organization is virtually nil. Your only recourse is to contract for a system to an outside computer systems development group. The basic user requirement is that the software is likely to remain in live operation for ten years or longer. After a couple of months' work, the requirements are ready to go out for bids. The system will be expensive, but you decide to award a contract to *two* competing system development groups. The need is so great that the system has to be good.
>
> A year later, both vendors have completed the project (which is a pleasant surprise). Skeptical of such serendipity, you have an outside adversary group run extensive testing on both systems. *Both* pieces of software meet your requirements and pass with flying colors. Now the dilemma: Which system should you put into operation?
>
> It occurs to you that maybe in the development of the software, a coarse golfer may be at work. So you call in both project managers and simply ask them to describe what happened during the system's development. The manager of Company A gives the following report:

"We think ours is a top-notch development group and your project represented our best effort. We reviewed your specifications and began work within two months. After only four months, we had a working version. In an effort to satisfy your needs exactly, we later uncovered a number of errors in the software. Over a period of months, these were slowly shaken out of the system until we were confident of system behavior.

"We checked the software constantly against your requirements, and, in doing so, we discovered a number of anomalies. You recall our asking you to clarify this situation a few months ago. Some of your clarifications required extensive changes, but we were determined to have the software meet your requirements. We put in quite a bit of overtime in the last two months to straighten everything out, and the shakedown has continued until this very day. Now we are confident that we have met both the letter and spirit of your project needs."

Impressive, you think. Had this been the only developer, there would be reason to think that the software could be installed with confidence.

Nevertheless, you ask the same question of the project manager of Company B. What happened during development?

"Our company prides itself on its reputation of proven techniques and I am delighted to tell you what happened. Ten months ago, in reviewing your user requirements in great detail, we called you about a number of anomalies that needed clarification. At this point, we could not have proceeded to write the detailed specification without the answers you provided for us. Later, we submitted our specification to our team of engineers who spent another three months on the design of the software.

"Time was slipping by quickly and we were beginning to be concerned about meeting the schedule. At this point, we made some preliminary tests with a rough prototype to check the behavior of the system and see how users would respond. This took another month.

"Three months ago, we began coding. We had just established a new procedure requiring that all repairs and changes to the software be recorded automatically. We were anxious to see how everything would work out. You know, every piece of code worked right the first time. Our final integration of the software was completed about three weeks before delivery. All the modules were combined into a final working unit, and no repairs were made. Even with only two weeks left for live testing, not a single change was required. The whole piece of software worked right the first time."

You are puzzled. Which piece of software would you choose—that of Company A or that of Company B?

This above scenario can be rephrased as follows: two pieces of software with identical behavior are error free, satisfy the user requirements completely, are equally efficient, and certified to be absolutely correct. The only difference you can find is ·that during development, one required extensive correction and modification and the other worked right the first time. The question is: Based only on this information, can we conclude that one piece of software is superior to the other?

To answer this question, two related issues need to be put into focus:

1. What is a correct program?

2. Is it even conceivable that a program could work correctly the first time?

What Is a Correct Program?

We often hear phrases like "it works" or "the program is now working." This doesn't always mean the same thing. Consider the following interpretations. (What follows is a list similar to that in [Conway et al., 1976] and [Marcotty and Ledgard, 1986].)

> *Compiler Correctness.* The program, when submitted to a compiler for the language or some similar processor, reports no diagnosed errors.

For some people it is remarkable that a program passes through the compiler without error. This level of correctness, however, is of little interest to the professional programmer. Any errors that can be detected by a compiler are usually minor. Moreover, since the compiler is a knowledgeable overseer, getting this level of correctness is easy. The next level of correctness, however, is not.

> *Runtime Correctness.* Execution proceeds from the beginning of the program to the end without any collapse of the program.

There is no expectation here whether the input or output is meaningful, but only that there are no problems that cause the program to crash. This level of correctness may be difficult to reach in a significant piece of software.

> *Programmer Correctness.* For a wide set of representative inputs, the programmer is satisfied with the output.

This is the definition most programmers use. Presumably there exists a range of possible inputs, intended or unintended, for which the program produces a response. The definition assumes that the user is allowed to enter certain inputs for which the program's only response may be an error message. But in no case must the message come from the underlying operating system. The boundary conditions, invalid inputs, and special cases are handled by the program itself.

Adversary Correctness. The program is subjected to all kinds of inputs in an attempt to make the program crash. The program still gives a reasonable response.

In this definition the hard cases are the ones that count. For example, the user may try to save a file twice, give no input when an item is expected, type a control key in response to a yes-no question, or give a burst of data so as to overflow the capacity of the program.

Specification Correctness. Given a clear, complete, and detailed specification of the program's behavior, the program acts correctly within the letter and spirit of the specification.

This significant step means that the behavior of the program is dictated by a written formal description. It is on this basis that software should be written.

User Correctness. The user judges what is correct. Here the program gives a predictable response (as judged by the user) to every conceivable input situation, including erroneous cases.

This is a subtle matter—the way users judge whether a piece of software works or not. For instance, suppose the user is entering text to a text editor and the editor issues a message along the lines "Memory Almost Exhausted". The user may continue to enter text and consider it an error if the program eventually crashes, although the program is working as it was designed. These kinds of cases form the gray line.

My own definition of a working program is as follows:

- There is no combination of inputs for which control passes to the underlying operating system to issue diagnostics.

- With a reasonable interpretation of the letter and the spirit of the specification (in whatever form it exists), the program's behavior matches that of the specification.

- There are no surprises. Boundary conditions, input quirks, and overloading of the program's resources are all cases the program handles in some reasonable manner.

Can It Be Done?

No one is foolish enough to believe that one can write large programs that work correctly the first time. Human limits certainly come into play. It is this admission that caused the title of this essay to include the word "third" rather than the more evocative word "first". So assume it is possible to come close, say, with only twenty or thirty corrected errors and changes in 10,000 lines of code. In practice this may seem to be an extraordinarily low error rate, though it does not include the numerous editing changes that go on when a program is being written or constructed.

To illustrate this point, consider the following method of counting errors:

> A programmer or programming team writes one of the software modules, perhaps a 50-line procedure or a 300-line package of procedures and supporting code. The module is reviewed and changed several times but is not submitted immediately for compilation or execution. After considerable review, the programming group believes that the module is, if not perfect, at least as good as can be written. The module is submitted to the compiler and the count starts. The count is incremented by 1 for each problem, anomaly, or change of behavior that must be fixed to make the program fully operational.

Next, suppose we have a team of four programmers and a utility program is needed, say, to copy files or to take a collection of data and draw a bar graph. Assume that the program will take five or six pages of code. The team member who is going to write the program studies the problem and comes up with an algorithm. At the next team walkthrough (a meeting to discuss work), the algorithm is shown briefly to other members of the team who offer their comments. The next day the programmer refines the algorithm so that the appropriate comments are taken into consideration. He then spends a day or so, part-time, writing the program. He is careful about program readability, uses good names and layout conventions, and produces a draft of the program. He submits this draft to the team members at the next walkthrough. Again, the team offers its comments about organization and general readability. The programmer then produces a revised draft, which is proofread by another team member to check its detailed structure and correctness. Finally, both team members are satisfied that the program does the entire job.

Is it reasonable to assume in this circumstance that the program might work correctly the first (or third) time? I think so. At least it is conceivable. The design and implementation of this program has had the benefit of a few other minds and the careful craftsmanship of a single author. If these procedures are followed, it is hard to imagine that there would be any serious errors. In fact, it would be reasonable to expect that the program would not need any modifications; it should compile and execute properly, and it should satisfy the requirements that were the objective of the program.

Now, what about a sizable piece of software? Imagine a piece of software that might be 10,000 lines long. Such a piece of software might take several months for a small team of professionals to complete. Suppose the project were started with a user requirement specification. From this, a preliminary user manual and functional specification of the entire piece of software were then derived. Assume also that the piece of software underwent, under the team's scrutiny, a careful design in the best software tradition, and that not a line of code (other than for prototype or test purposes) was written until the complete test set was defined as well. In short, assume that the project followed a clear and well-planned lifecycle.

When it comes time for the code to be written, imagine the same scenario as outlined earlier for our smaller utility where modules are defined, written, checked, and rechecked, that is, the software grows slowly in a top-down fashion. For the larger program, is it conceivable that a good portion of the software could work correctly the first time? I think that in these circumstances it is at least conceivable. So many defenses have been made against change, so many defenses have been made to define the problem, and so much human interaction over the technical aspects of the project has taken place that the possibility of error is enormously reduced.

In the professional world, life is often not as simple, although frequently there are too many excuses for complexity. Also, larger software projects call for even tighter controls and greater imagination. But we do not simply get code to work correctly the first time by applying well-defined programming standards or last minute code-reading procedures. This issue stems from the very beginning of the software project. Errors are not, generally speaking, accidents. They are cumulative results of many aspects of the software lifecycle. Correct code is not good luck—it is a matter of preparation.

Why Attempt It?

So why in the world would anyone *attempt* to write programs that work correctly the first time rather than, say, start by using a compiler check as a kind of editing tool? On efficiency grounds (that is, efficiency of the project's resources and time) we can well argue that the matter is a draw. It is probably just as efficient in the short run to use the best software development techniques in the first place. Yes, it does take more time up front to prepare our thinking, consolidate our design, write drafts of the program, redraft it based on the opinions of others, and so on. But the benefits come down on the side of the professional programmer. These benefits separate him or her from the P-sub-A or even the coarse programmer.

I don't think I've met a programmer who really understands how much time evaporates on the terminal. As soon as the first glimmer of a version appears, the rush is to the terminal, the compiler, and the runtime system. Errors are found and simply hacked out. Odd cases are discovered and these are added in, corrected, and revised. The programmer comes away thinking that his Trojan exertions at the terminal are heroic efforts to right a program gone wrong.

In my opinion, most of this terminal time is a complete waste. Cases where a ten-page module of a piece of software are compiled and run a hundred times are not uncommon. Think of the complexity of dealing with the files and the various versions, the time spent logging into the computer, getting into the editor, making the changes, recompiling, and rerunning. Think of all the keystrokes, the waiting for the compiler and the runtime system to finish their jobs, the execution of code that is already working, just to get to the part that is not working. My point is simply that more time spent before coding saves the equivalent amount of time during verification and testing.

I do not at all wish to imply that the terminal should not be used for editing. Indeed, it should. Drafts can be written, edited, re-edited, and edited many times over as each version is refined. Nor do I wish to argue against prototype software, seeing if ideas work, top-down testing, or developing a program in small units. The point is that the compiler and runtime system should be the Supreme Court and used only when a program unit is truly ready.

The most powerful argument, though, is one of quality. The attempt to write a piece of software that might work right the first time involves a significant human effort to promote *human* understanding of the software. At each step of the preparation before the first run, more and more elements of quality must be added as a natural result of a careful process. Care, deliberation, and concentration are peaked. The quality of code grows with each refinement of the initial idea; from the first design, each special case or spurious input is accounted for beforehand. As the process of trying to achieve this result becomes more serious, more quality is naturally injected into the process. Sometimes the attempt may fail, and bugs and changes will arise. But the closer we come to this goal, the higher the intrinsic quality of the final program.

Quality up front is an idea whose time has come, at last, to more than just the programming profession in America. In a recent *New York Times* article (March 3, 1985), David A. Garvin makes a succinct remark that I like: "Quality is free." The giant industries in the United States (IBM, General Motors, and Allegheny Ludlum Steel) realize how expensive it is to recall an automobile or replace a unit when all that might have been done was to build the car right the first time or to replace a defective part rather than have to perform major surgery to replace the larger component unit.

Spending time hacking away at the terminal is just another way of laying your fourth putt dead. Yes, the ball will eventually go in the hole, but what a waste of time. Looking back at choosing between the two companies, the imagination cannot be stretched too much to think of how much more quality must intrinsically be patterned into the program of Company B because—it worked right the first time.

The Culture of Pascal

Standard Pascal for Would-Be Experts

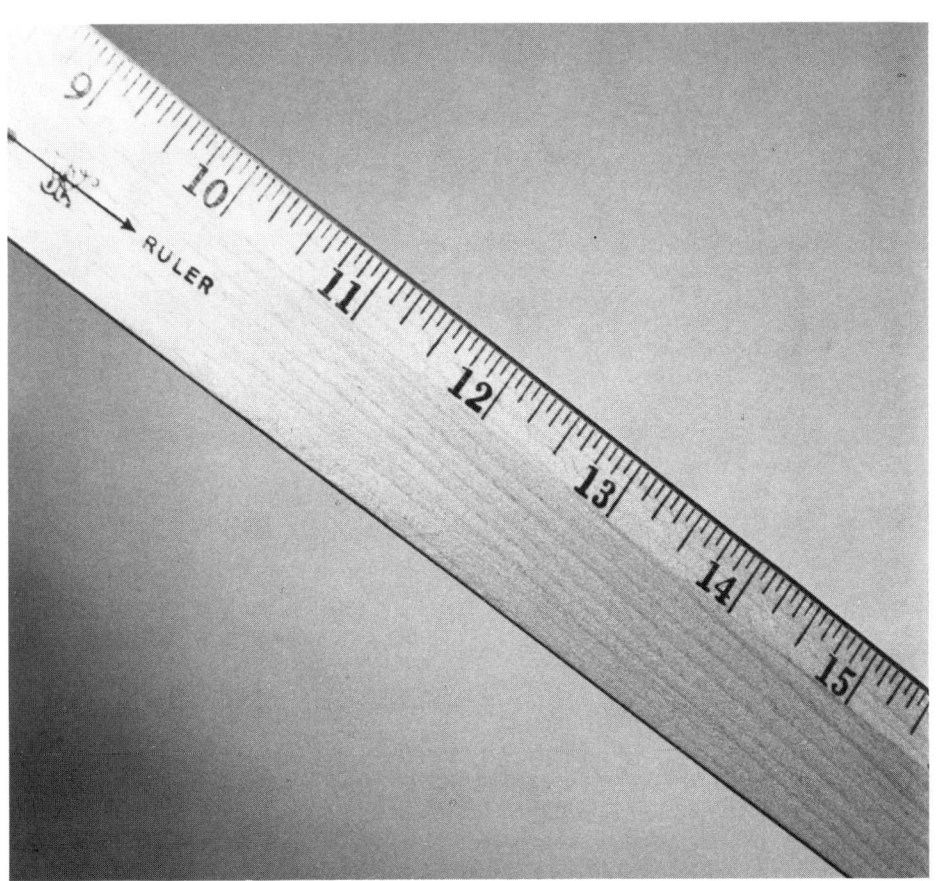

Every language has its subtle corners. Pascal is no exception. Portions of the definition of Standard Pascal are quite hard to understand. There are features in the language that few are aware of. For some, there are surprises. A program fragment that looks innocuous may turn out to be invalid. A program fragment that looks absurd may turn out quite respectable.

There are probably few implementations of Pascal that actually conform to the letter of the standard definition of Pascal. Nevertheless, Pascal is defined by a standard and it is this standard to which we turn here. We will look at some of Pascal's features that perhaps the reader has not appreciated or understood. The intent here is to search out some of these corners of Pascal and illuminate them with examples.

Naming Issues

We start with the observation that Pascal has both reserved keywords and predefined names. The words "begin" and "end" are keywords. The words "INPUT", "INTEGER", and "READ" are predefined names. (*Note:* Upper- and lower-case letters are considered equivalent.) With this in mind, consider then the following little program:

```
program PREDEFINEDNAMES (INPUT, OUTPUT);

   { -- Can BOOLEAN be INTEGER?}
   type
      BOOLEAN = INTEGER;
   var
      R: BOOLEAN;
      READ: REAL;

begin
   READLN (R);
   READ := 3.14 * (R * R);
   WRITELN (READ)
end.
```

Is this program valid? Ridiculous, yes, but is it valid?

To understand this program we must be aware of the scope rules for predefined names. The predefined names denote the required constants, types, procedures, and functions in Pascal. For instance, TRUE and FALSE are required constants, and READ and DISPOSE are required procedures. These predefined names fall under the normal scope rules for Pascal, with the understanding that these names have a scope as if they were defined in a region enclosing the program itself. The reason for this rule is to allow programmers to give a new meaning for some predefined name. For example, a programmer might want to overwrite the standard definition of the procedure READ. Whether this is a good idea or not is a matter we shall not take up here. We only note that it is possible.

So, in the above program, we see a type definition in which the name BOOLEAN is identified with the type INTEGER; and READ is introduced as a variable name of type REAL. The program thus is perfectly valid. It simply reads in the integer value of the radius of a circle and prints out the area of a circle as a real number.

Another subtlety of the scope rules is illustrated in the following example:

```
program IDENTICALNAMES(INPUT, OUTPUT);

    { -- Are both definitions of X valid? }
    var
       PAIR: record
                 X: INTEGER;
                 Y: INTEGER
             end;
         X, Y: CHAR;

begin
    PAIR.X := 1;
    X      := '%';
    WRITELN (X, PAIR.X)
end.
```

The question here is whether X can be declared a component of a record and a simple variable. The answer is yes. The reason lies in Pascal's scope rules for record types and record variables. In the type definition of a record structure, the occurrence of an identifier as the name of a record component defines a scope for the identifier which is the component list of the record definition itself. Thus other declarations of the same identifier outside the record definition are allowed. Similarly, when a record variable (like PAIR) is used, the scope of the identifiers for the components of the record variable is "opened up." In this way, the preceding program is also perfectly valid.

Now let us visit a similar problem for enumeration types. Consider the following sequence:

```
type
    CONTROLCHAR = (ACK, BELL, NULL);
    CMDOPTION   = (UP, DOWN, NULL);
var
    CH:  CONTROLCHAR;
    ARG: CMDOPTION;
 ...

CH := NULL;
```

As is well known in Pascal, these two type declarations cannot exist together. In particular, the name NULL is assumed to be declared twice and is thus invalid. Note that the assignment

```
CH := NULL
```

is thus invalid, even though from its context we can determine that NULL denotes a control character and not a command option. All of this stems from the rule that an identifier declared as an enumeration type has a scope that is similar to the type names and variable names declared in the same declarative sequence. Thus multiple uses of the same name are not allowed.

All of this may not be satisfactory. There is a general difficulty when different enumeration types have values that are denoted by the same identifier. One possible resolution to this problem is to declare the different enumeration types with different scope levels. For instance, consider the following example:

```
program NAMECONFLICT (INPUT, OUTPUT);

    { -- Are both type declarations valid? }
    type
       CONTROLCHAR = (ACK, BELL, NULL);
    var
       CH: CONTROLCHAR;

    procedure NESTED:
       type
          CMDOPTION = (UP, DOWN, NULL);
       ...
       CH := NULL  { -- statement 1 }
    end;

begin
    ...
    CH := NULL;  { -- statement 2 }
    ...
end.
```

Here, both type declarations are, indeed, valid. At the outer level, NULL denotes a control character; at the inner level, NULL denotes a command option. But the problem is not over. The statement

```
CH := NULL  { -- statement 1 }
```

is invalid. NULL is of type CMDOPTION, and CH is of type CONTROLCHAR. Thus the new enumeration effectively hides the identical names of an enclosing enumeration type.

Is there a way around this? Consider another crack at the problem:

```
program RESOLVECONFLICT (INPUT, OUTPUT);

   type
      CONTROLCHAR = (ACK, BELL, NULL);

   var
      CH: CONTROLCHAR;

   procedure NESTED;
     const
        NULLCH = NULL;
     type
        CMDOPTION = (UP, DOWN, NULL);
     ...
     CH := NULLCH  { -- statement 1 }
   end;

begin
   ...
   CH := NULL;
   ...
end.
```

This rendering is also invalid. It appears that the constant declaration of NULL, which precedes the type declaration of CMDOPTION, would make the identifier NULL of type CONTROLCHAR. When the type declaration for CMDOPTION is introduced immediately after, a new definition of NULL is introduced, whose scope is the entire block. Hence, the assignment

```
CH := NULLCH  { -- statement 1 }
```

is not valid, and neither is the declaration of NULLCH. The only real solution is to rename NULL in the outer block.

With Statements

Few programmers get heavily entangled in with statements, for these too have their own subtleties of scope and naming. In Pascal, with statements may be nested within each other, and a with statement may also have several record variables in a single with clause. Although it might be argued that this kind of power is hardly necessary in a language like Pascal, these possibilities exist.

The problem is that, in the body of a with statement, record components appear as normal variables. For instance, the statement

```
    WRITELN (X);
```

can refer to a variable, here X, which is not a simple variable, but a component of
a record structure. The programmer must make the association between the
variable and the component of a particular record. In order to do this, the with
clause in an enclosing with statement must be used to resolve the naming
situation.

With this in mind, let us look at the program of Figure 12.1. This is a tricky
example, so we will treat it on a line-by-line basis. The game is to figure out which
seven values are printed by the program.

Figure 12.1 *Use of With Statements*

```
program WITHSTM (INPUT, OUTPUT);

    type
        COORDINATE =
            record
                X: REAL;
                Y: REAL;
            end;
        LINE:
            record
                START: COORDINATE;
                STOP : COORDINATE
            end;

    var
        X: REAL;
        POINT1, POINT2: COORDINATE;
        SIDE1, SIDE2: LINE;

begin
    X := 0.0;
    POINT1.X := 1.0;
    POINT1.Y := 2.0;
    POINT2.X := 3.0;
    POINT2.Y := 4.0;

    SIDE1.START := POINT1;
    SIDE1.STOP   := POINT2;

    SIDE2.START.X := 5.0;
    SIDE2.START.Y := 6.0;
    SIDE2.STOP.X   := 7.0;
    SIDE2.STOP.Y   := 8.0;
```

Figure 12.1 *continued*

```
{ -- what 7 values are printed? }
with POINT1 do
   WRITELN (X);

with POINT1, POINT2 do
   WRITELN (X);

with POINT1.X do
   WRITELN (X);

with SIDE1 do
   WRITELN (X);

with SIDE1, START do
   WRITELN (X);

with START, SIDE1 do
   WRITELN (X);

with SIDE1.START do
   WRITELN (X);

end.
```

The first case is easy.

```
with POINT1 do
   WRITELN(X);
```

Here the value POINT1.X is printed, which gives the value 1.0. This is a conventional use of a with statement.

Now let us look at the next example.

```
with POINT1, POINT2 do
   WRITELN(X);
```

Here there are two qualifying record variables. According to the rules of Pascal, this is equivalent to

```
with POINT1 do
   with POINT2 do
      WRITELN(X);
```

So, POINT2 qualifies X and thus the value 3.0 is printed.

The next one is a bit odd.

```
with POINT1.X do
    WRITELN(X);
```

There is no substructure to POINT1.X, hence, the with clause itself is invalid. Note that the X in the WRITELN statement is unqualified. It refers to the simple variable X, which has the value 0.0.

Next consider

```
with SIDE1 do
    WRITELN(X);
```

SIDE1 opens the scope for its components START and STOP. Neither of these qualify X. Hence 0.0 is printed again.

With the next example,

```
with SIDE1, START do
    WRITELN(X);
```

SIDE1 qualifies the record variable START, which, in turn, qualifies X. This means that the X in the WRITELN statement is, in fact, SIDE1.START.X. Hence the value 1.0 is printed.

Reversing the two, as in

```
with START, SIDE1 do
    WRITELN(X);
```

produces no effect on X as far as qualification is concerned, but it is invalid. START by itself is not a record variable.

In the last example,

```
with SIDE1.START do
    WRITELN(X);
```

X is qualified by a compound name, which does apply to X and which results in the value 1.0 being printed. Tricky? Yes.

Type Issues

The Pascal type system, by and large, is carefully crafted. For its time of invention, many years ago, the type model was a landmark.

Standard Pascal does not come with a predefined type for strings. Strings are considered, instead, to be "packed" arrays of characters. Strings are packed for economy of storage. They are also arrays in that the properties of arrays can be used to reference and update elements of a string. Whether or not this is a good model for strings is not an issue we address here. It is just the way it is.

Figure 12.2 is an sample program using strings. The program poses a number of questions. The first question is: Which of the following are valid string assignments?

```
PURESTRVAR    := 'ABCD';
LETTERSTRVAR := 'ABCD';
CHARSTRVAR    := 'ABCD';
```

In this case, only the first assignment is valid. The packed array of the letters A through Z is not considered a string because its component type is not of type CHAR, but rather a subtype consisting of only letters. The third assignment is not valid because the array is not packed.

Following these assignments is a conditional statement. Which branch is taken? According to the standard, the actual branch taken is implementation defined. The standard takes no position on whether the lower-case letters precede the upper-case letters in the ordering of characters for a particular implementation.

In the assignments following the conditional statement, none of the combinations is valid. The reason? First of all, the left and right sides of each assignment are values of different named types. Although Pascal does not keep such a rule religiously, the only allowed assignment between *string* types are those that have the same number of components. Aside from this, assignment to array variables is only allowed if the arrays have the same type.

The final portion of this program employs a function applied to different variables. These are as follows:

```
N := NUMBLANKS(PURESTRVAR);
N := NUMBLANKS(LETTERSTRVAR);
N := NUMBLANKS(CHARSTRVAR)
```

Which of these are valid? The first is valid simply because the type of the argument and the type of the parameter are the same. The following two are not valid. An argument must be assignment compatible with the type specified by the parameter, which is not the case.

The kinds of issues we have raised are just as strict when functions or procedures themselves are used as parameters. Consider the following sequence:

```
type
    LETTER = 'A'..'Z';
    NEWLETTER = LETTER;
var
    RESULT: CHAR;

procedure APPLY (function F(L: LETTER): CHAR; var C: Char);
    var
        NEWCHAR: CHAR;
```

```
begin
  READ (NEWCHAR);
  C := F(NEWCHAR)  { -- is this call valid? }
end
```

Here we have a procedure APPLY, one of whose parameters is a function that takes a LETTER as an argument and returns a value of type CHAR. The first question is: Is the statement

```
C := F(NEWCHAR)
```

valid? The answer is yes. The reason is that, although the parameter L and the argument NEWCHAR are of different types, they are assignment compatible because one is a subrange of the other.

Now suppose we had defined the following functions:

```
function PARENT (C: CHAR): CHAR;
function SAME (L: LETTER): LETTER;
function EQUAL (NL: NEWLETTER): CHAR;
```

With these definitions, consider the following calls to the procedure APPLY:

```
APPLY (PARENT, RESULT);
APPLY (SAME, RESULT);
APPLY (EQUAL, RESULT);
```

Which of these are valid?

To answer this, look at the definition of Pascal and the rules governing when a function argument is an acceptable match for a function parameter. These rules are rather strict. You must ask if the parameter list for the function argument is "congruous" with the parameter list of the function parameter. The rules for congruity of two formal parameter lists require that they be almost identical. For instance, they must have the same number of parameters, the same type identifier for each parameter, the same number of parameter sections, and the same result type (in the case of functions). In the preceding cases, the function PARENT is not valid because its parameter is of type CHAR and not of type LETTER. The function SAME is not valid because its result is of type LETTER and not CHAR. The function EQUAL, however, is valid because the type NEWLETTER is associated with type LETTER. A bit tricky? Yes.

Variant Records

One area that seems to cause confusion in Pascal is the subject of variant records. This is not exactly a feature of Pascal that is used by the uninitiated. Variant records are much more in the domain of the compiler writer and the system

Figure 12.2 *Using Strings*

```pascal
program STRINGS (INPUT, OUTPUT);

   type
      PURESTR   = packed array[1..4] of CHAR;
      LETTERSTR = packed array[1..4] of 'A'..'Z';
      CHARSTR   = array[1..4] of CHAR;

   var
      PURESTRVAR: PURESTR;
      LETTERSTRVAR: LETTERSTR;
      CHARSTRVAR: CHARSTR;
      N: INTEGER;

function NUMBLANKS (S: PURESTR): INTEGER;
   ...
end;

begin
   { -- Which are valid? }
   PURESTRVAR := 'ABCD';
   LETTERSTRVAR := 'ABCD';
   CHARSTRVAR := 'ABCD';

   { -- Which branch is taken? }
   if 'abcd' < 'ABCD' then
      WRITELN (1)
   else
      WRITELN (2);

   { -- Which are valid? }
   PURESTRVAR := LETTERSTRVAR;
   LETTERSTRVAR := CHARSTRVAR;
   CHARSTRVAR := PURESTRVAR;
   PURESTRVAR := CHARSTRVAR;

   { -- Which calls are valid? }
   N := NUMBLANKS(PURESTRVAR);
   N := NUMBLANKS(LETTERSTRVAR);
   N := NUMBLANKS(CHARSTRVAR);

end.
```

programmer. Nevertheless, variant records seem to draw the attention of many programmers, whether they use them or not.

Figure 12.3 illustrates some of the Pascal rules for variant records. In particular, this program defines a type named **POLICYINFO** as a record type with three variants in its variant part. The algorithm portion of the program asks several questions. The first question is: In, for instance,

```
POLICY1.KIND := AUTO;
```

can one assign to the tag field? This is perfectly acceptable Pascal and sets up AUTO as the active variant. Once this variant is established, the components of the other variants become inaccessible. Hence the statement

```
POLICY1.NUMPERSONS := 5;
```

is not valid.

Note also that if no variant is active in the given record, the components of the record variant cannot be used until a tag field is set. Thus

```
POLICY2.COLOR := BLUE;
```

is not valid.

There are two ways to change the active variant. One is to assign another value to the tag field; the other is via a complete record assignment, which overwrites the previously active variant with an entirely new record value. Hence the statement

```
POLICY2 := POLICY1;
```

is valid and establishes **POLICY2** as a record value with the same variant as **POLICY1**. Similarly one can overwrite the tag field itself, as in

```
POLICY2.KIND := HOME;
```

This assignment renders the fields of the previously active variant as undefined.

Evaluation Effects

Most programs change the mapping from variables to values through explicit assignments. Expressions, which are used to compute variables, normally do not alter the state. However, Pascal, like most languages, allows side effects in expressions. For this reason, spurious cases can arise where the evaluation order can have subtle effects. The definition of Standard Pascal tries to rule out such cases, or, at the least, leaves such cases to be defined by the implementation.

Figure 12.3 *Use of Variant Records*

```pascal
program VARIANTS(INPUT, OUTPUT);

    type
        POLICYTYPE = (AUTO, HOME, HEALTH);
        POLICYINFO =
            record
                POLICYNUM: INTEGER;
                HOLDER:    PERSONNAME;
                case KIND: POLICYTYPE of
                    AUTO: (MAKE:  COMPANYNAME;
                           YEAR:  INTEGER;
                           COLOR: COLORCODE;
                           REGISTRATION: INTEGER);
                    HOME: (DESIGN:   DESIGNAME;
                           VALUE:    INTEGER;
                           LOCATION: LOCATIONINFO);
                    HEALTH: (NUMPERSONS: INTEGER;
                             MEDHISTORY: MEDICALINFO)
            end;
        DATAFILE: file of POLICYINFO;
    var
        POLICY1, POLOCY2, POLICY3: POLICYINFO;

begin
    POLICY1.POLICYNUM := 765567;
    POLICY2.POLICYNUM := 123321;

    { -- Can one assign to the tag field? }
    POLICY1.KIND := AUTO;

    { -- Can a variant be violated? }
    POLICY1.NUMPERSONS := 5;

    { -- Can one assign to a component with no tag set? }
    POLICY2.COLOR := BLUE;

    { -- Can one overwrite a variant? }
    POLICY2 := POLICY1;

    { -- Can one change a variant? }
    POLICY2.KIND := HOME;

end.
```

Consider the following program.

```
program RESETFILE(F);

    var
        F: TEXT;
        C: CHAR

procedure SIDESWIPE (var F1: TEXT; var C1: CHAR);
begin
    RESET (F1);
    WRITE (C1);
    C1 := F1↑
end;

begin
    READ (F, C);
    SIDESWIPE (F, F↑)
end.
```

Strictly speaking, this program is in error and the violation should be reported at runtime. Where is the error? The problem comes in with the call

```
SIDESWIPE (F, F↑)
```

Here the file F and its corresponding buffer variable F↑ are passed as arguments. Inside the procedure SIDESWIPE, the file F is reset while the reference to the buffer variable still exists. Whether most implementations check for this case is problematic. Note that if C1 is not a var parameter, the program is fine.

Next consider the following example:

```
program EVALUATIONORDER (INPUT, OUTPUT);

    var
        A: INTEGER;

function INCREMENT (var I: INTEGER): INTEGER;
begin
    I := I + 1;
    INCREMENT := I
end;

function ADD (X, Y: INTEGER): INTEGER;
begin
    ADD := X + Y
end;
```

```
begin
  A := 2;
  A := ADD (INCREMENT(A), A);
  WRITE (A);    { -- What is printed? }

  A := 2;
  A := INCREMENT(A) + A;
  WRITELN (A)   { -- What is printed? }
end.
```

Here we have a function INCREMENT that produces a side effect to its argument. This function is called twice in the program, once as a argument to the function ADD and once as an expression that adds two values. What is printed? It depends. Possible answers are

```
5 5
5 6
6 5
6 6
```

Each of these interpretations is valid for Pascal. Pascal leaves the order of evaluation for arithmetic expressions and the order for evaluation for the arguments in an argument list up to the implementation. Obviously it is unwise to write such programs.

Finally, a small point. The parameters of a program need not be files, although this is by far the normal case. Thus the program

```
program PROGRAMPARAMETERS (N1, N2);
  var
      N1, N2: INTEGER;
begin
  if N1 > 3 then
      N2 := 0
  else
      N2 := 1
end.
```

is perfectly valid.

Some Syntactic Points

Although matters of pure syntax tend to be the easy parts of a language to understand and use, a few corners of Pascal syntax deserve mentioning. Consider the following program.

```
program SYNTAXERRORS(INPUT, OUTPUT);

    type
      REC = record
                { nothing }
              end;

    var
      A: array[1..3] of INTEGER;
      B: array[1..3] of INTEGER;

      RANGE: 1.0..10.0;
      R: REC;

begin
    A[1] := 1.0;
    A[2] := 2.0;
    A[3] := 3.0;
    B := A;
    RANGE := 4.0
end.
```

There are some syntactic errors in this program. First, we ask: Can the field list in a record type be empty? The answer is yes, and the definition of the type REC is perfectly valid, although useless. Second, we ask: Can the ranges for the variable RANGE be given as real quantities? The answer is no. This is an error. Third, the assignment

```
B := A;
```

is not valid. Because A and B have distinct type definitions, even though identical, the assignment has a type error.

What about comments? Consider the following:

```
{ -- Will this comment appear on the compiler listing? }
program COMMENTS (INPUT, OUTPUT);

    var
      I, J, TOTAL: INTEGER;

begin
    READLN (I);
    TOTAL: := 0;
    if I < 100 then
      for J := 1 to I do { products }
          TOTAL := TOTAL + I
    else
```

```
   { -- Can this code be commented out?
   for J := 1 to I do  { sums }
      TOTAL := TOTAL + I };

 WRITELN (TOTAL)

end.  { -- Will the missing brace be caught?
```

For this program, the following observations hold:

- The comment preceding the program header is valid. Pascal treats this comment as a single space and is part of the program.

- The comment immediately following the **else** is invalid. In particular, comments cannot be used to block out code that itself contains a comment. Pascal takes the brace following the word sums as the closing brace for the comment beginning after the keyword **else**.

- The comment at the end of the program is a tossup. The Pascal standard does not define whether this is an acceptable comment or not. It is left to the implementation.

Finally, it is hard to close the matter of Standard Pascal without at least touching once upon the semicolon issue. Consider the following program.

```
program BADSEMICOLONS (INPUT, OUTPUT);

   type
      REC =
         record
            X: INTEGER;;
         end;

   var
      V: 1..4;

begin
   READLN(V);;
   case V of
      1: WRITELN (V);;
      2: ;
      3: ;
   end;;
end.
```

There are certainly too many semicolons in the program, but how do they square up?

- The pair of semicolons in the record declaration is not valid. Although the field list of a record structure may be empty and a semicolon can be placed after each component definition, the extra semicolon is invalid.

- The pair of semicolons after the call to READLN is valid. Pascal allows an empty statement (which is invisible) to be inserted between the two semicolons.

- The pair of semicolons after the WRITELN is not valid. Only one semicolon can appear after each alternative of the case statement.

- The semicolons after the case options 2 and 3 are valid. An empty statement is assumed for each alternative.

- The pair of semicolons after the word **end** is valid. Again, an empty statement can be put here.

Although such rules may provide some curiosity, it is hardly an exciting game to discover exactly where semicolons must or must not appear.

This ends our little tour of the darker corners of Pascal. Obviously, implementations may deviate from the standard definition, especially on the points raised here. Although our tour of Pascal has taken us places where the professional programmer would never want to tread, understanding one's language to such a degree is certainly a great advantage. A professional programmer should know the language extraordinarily well.

13

Pascal Idiosyncracies

Professional programmers choose their tools carefully. They understand how they work, what is good about them, and what is not. The most important tool, of course, is the programming language.

I have heard it said that every programming language has the same number of mistakes per acre. Although the acreage of Pascal is smaller than some languages, I believe that Pascal is no exception. Its deficiencies are more a matter of detail than of any broad shortcoming of the language. Not all languages suffer from this sort of problem. For instance, Ada's main shortcoming is its large scale, which, I believe, could have been avoided by saying no to the thirst for more and more features. Its design, however, is most elegant. The language LISP has a consistent design, although its syntax readily becomes opaque.

Remember that Pascal was designed years ago, when language design issues were emerging at a rapid rate and many of the topics we think about today were not well understood. This makes it easy to be critical, for hindsight is always the easiest method. Since Pascal has been taken far beyond its original objectives as a teaching language, it deserves a closer look.

Case Statements

The idea of a case statement, originally proposed by Hoare [Hoare, 1981], is one of the clearest control structures to emerge in contemporary programming. The idea behind the case statement is that there is a controlling variable that can take on one of several discrete values. Based on the actual value of the controlling variable, an action (or sequence of actions) is selected for execution. In its basic conception, the idea is easy to implement and a pleasure to read.

In practice, however, the case statement in Pascal is quite impotent. It suffers from a number of practical flaws that make its utility not as wide reaching as it could be.

A first missing feature of the case statement is the ability to use a subrange as a choice in a case statement. For example, consider

```
case MENUNUM of
   1:   SAVEITEM (ITEM);
   2:   GETITEM (ITEM);
   3..9: RECORDOPTIONS (ITEM);
  10:   CLEARDISPLAY
end
```

Here instead of requiring that 3, 4, 5, 6, 7, 8, and 9 be listed explicitly, as is required in Standard Pascal, the range 3..9 is given. This is typical whenever we have one or more ranges of contiguous values and each range calls for a single action.

A second but related problem comes when we have again a rather large range of choices—a few result in special actions and all the rest fall into a single category. This gives rise the idea of an "otherwise" or an "else" alternative for a case statement. Consider the following:

```
case INITIALCHAR of
   'A'..'Z': READID (SYMBOL)
   '0'..'9': READNUM (SYMBOL)
   else:     REPORTERROR (ODDCHAR)
end
```

The meaning here is that the else option stands for all choices not explicitly listed. This feature, when combined with subranges, gives the case statement a much greater latitude in handling practical problems.

Strings as Arrays

There is a certain thinking that identifies character strings with arrays. In Pascal, for instance, a string or string type is a packed array whose smallest index value is 1 and which has at least two elements. The normal operations on arrays also apply to character strings. For example, we can reference a character in a string just as we do for a component in an array, and we can assign characters to the components of an array to create new strings.

I don't buy it. Strings are not arrays. Conceptually, an array is like a table, a collection of individual items. A string is different. Strings behave partly like integers in that their subparts are not always relevant. An integer stands for itself. So does a string. Of course, with some strings it makes sense to look at its third character or to change a character to another character, but these operations are significant only when we are doing string manipulation. The basic operations on strings are reading, printing, concatenation, and comparison (for example, to see which of two strings is alphabetically first). There are strings with one character and, of course, a null string (a string of no characters). If strings were viewed solely as a type of their own, they would not be particularly akin to arrays.

In Pascal, stretching the concept of a string into that of an array certainly has its odd moments. To start with, a null array is hard to explain. We can define and name string constants. This is all well and good, but we cannot define constant arrays with noncharacter components. Even if we could, certainly the syntax would not look at all like that of a string. The predefined procedure WRITE cannot be applied to values of structured types (for example, records, arrays, or sets), yet the procedure is defined to operate on string types. Similarly, the relational operators cannot be applied to structured types, but they can be applied to strings.

The matter gets more complicated when we bring in the issue of packed. In Pascal, strings must be declared as *packed* arrays. There are restrictions in the language prohibiting the use of packed arrays in certain situations and there are predefined procedures for converting between packed and unpacked structures.

There would be little reason for strings to be explicitly packed if it were not for the recognition that most strings are not dissected into their parts, but are treated more as atomic elements. All this leads again to the simple point that strings are not arrays.

Unraveling With Statements

In Pascal, the with statement is a means of avoiding lengthy references to the components of a record structure. In its intent it is simple. For example, instead of writing

```
if (TODAY.MONTH = 12) and (TODAY.DAY = 31) then
   begin
      TODAY.YEAR  := TODAY.YEAR + 1;
      TODAY.MONTH := 1;
      TODAY.DAY   := 1
   end
else
   TODAY.DAY := TODAY.DAY + 1
```

We can instead write

```
with TODAY do
   if (MONTH = 12) and (DAY = 31) then
      begin
         YEAR  := YEAR + 1;
         MONTH := 1
         DAY   := 1
      end
   else
      DAY := DAY + 1
```

So much for the easy part.

In practice, the context in which the with statement is useful is vastly different from the preceding example. Professional programs often involve a number of different kinds of variables with different kinds of types.

Consider the following scenario:

```
with SYMBOL do begin
   ADVANCELINE (LEADINGLINES);

   if (LINEPOSITION + LEADINGSPACES > RIGHTEDGE)
   or (NAME = COMMENTSYM) then
      LINEPOSITION := LINEPOSITION + LEADINGSPACES
   else
      LINEPOSITION := MARGIN;
```

```
    if (LINEPOSITION + LENGTH > RIGHTEDGE) then
        begin
            SKIPLINE;
            if (MARGIN + LENGTH > RIGHTEDGE) then
                LINEPOSITION := 0
            else
                LINEPOSITION := MARGIN
        end;
    PRINTSYMBOL (VALUE, LENGTH, LINEPOSITION);
        ...
    end
```

The question here is: Which names does SYMBOL qualify? If it leaves you guessing, it does me, too. To find out, we have to refer to the declaration of SYMBOL, obtain its type, and look at the record structure of the type. This definition is often pages away.

It is easy to see a piece of program text with references to record structures and then imagine the text using a corresponding with statement, as in the simple pair of examples given earlier. But the program reader must do the opposite. Given a fragment of code without explicit references to record structures, the reader must determine which ones have the record qualification. To really decipher the piece of code, the reader usually ends up doing a good deal of page flipping to reference the relevant record type.

Program Organization

Pascal requires that a procedure must be declared before it is called. As a result, the so-called "main program" (that is, statements that are executed to start the program) appears at the very end. In between lie all the procedures. This in itself is less than optimal. Normally, we read the constant, type, and variable declarations for the program and then wish to read the main program.

Now suppose that the main program calls two or three procedures out of, say, twenty or fifty in the entire program. The procedures probably occur near the end of the program listing, so the programmer in a sense ends up reading the program backwards. The main program is on the last page, the first called procedures may be two, three, or ten pages back. Yet the declarations of the types and constants still appear on the very first few pages of the program. As a result the general reading style is sort of outside-in, with considerable page flipping.

If we add yet still another possibility in Pascal, that of nesting procedures within procedures, the problem is compounded significantly. In these cases begin-end block for a procedure can be separated from its local constant, type, and variable declarations by several pages. As I mentioned earlier, I don't recommend using this practice, and this is yet another reason.

We can circumvent this kind of dilemma by using procedures that are declared as "forward". Pascal allows us to declare the heading for a procedure and to state that its body is given later. The procedure body can then be introduced at more strategic places in the code. It is a bit unfortunate here that the full procedure header, which must include all the parameters of the procedure, is not repeated where the body is given. We can circumvent this with a comment describing the parameters, but this requires considerable discipline. In addition, it is not exactly clear how to print this information again.

Most programmers do not make much use of forward declarations. Procedures declared as forward were basically introduced to handle mutually recursive procedures, where forward declarations are a necessity. All in all there is no completely satisfactory solution to this dilemma. It is clearly an example where "declaration before use" as an idea breaks down.

Identifiers and Proportional Spacing

It has always struck me that Standard Pascal does not have a break character for identifiers. We must write, for instance, names like

```
PAGENUM
NEWENTRY
NEXTITEM
TRACKCONTROL
PERFORMREQUEST
GETREQUESTSTATUS
READANDPROCESSCARD
```

How much nicer these would be with a break character, as in

```
PAGE_NUM
NEW_ENTRY
NEXT_ITEM
TRACK_CONTROL
PERFORM_REQUEST
GET_REQUEST_STATUS
READ_AND_PROCESS_CARD
```

The improvement in readability is sharp and clear.

Some argue that a break character can be confusing because we might not know whether the break character itself were significant in determining the difference between identifiers. Thus opponents might argue that cases like

```
ITEM1      ITEM_12      NO_WHERE
ITEM_1     ITEM_1_2     NOW_HERE
```

are confusing. Should the pairs of identifiers be considered as different or the same? This argument baffles me, much like the tail wagging the dog. The break character, which in the preceding examples is an underscore, should be considered significant. Even still, cases like this are most certainly rare. The tricky cases almost never come up in practice. The 99% case is a simple identifier with individual compound parts. I cannot see any solid argument against a break character.

A break character in compound identifiers is quite common in natural languages (except German). In English we use the hyphen to separate the parts of compound words, for example,

Two-thirds
Hand-to-mouth
Non-skier
Well-known
Go-ahead

This convention is itself a strong reason to adopt a break character in identifiers. We might quibble over the choice of the break character itself, but that is not the issue—a break character is a good idea.

The absence of a break character in Pascal has led to several questionable methods to try to make programs more readable. None of them is really satisfactory. With all approaches there is a tendency for short identifiers (which is good), but often the tendency goes too far. My own preference is to put all keywords in lower case and everything else in upper case, for example,

```
while COUNT > N do begin
   DOTHIS;
   DOTHAT;
   DOTHEOTHER
end
```

This approach allows identifiers to have a higher visual aspect than keywords. I think this is the right idea because, in reading programs, the keywords eventually drift into the background for the programmer, especially when boldface is not available. Keywords generally serve as markers for a given construct. The focus is always the identifiers; these are the items that count. My preferred scheme, however, suffers a bit when identifiers get especially lengthy because all upper-case letters causes a reading strain. Since we should avoid identifiers that are too long as a general practice, this debit can be reduced (but not eliminated).

An approach that is gaining increasing vogue is printing identifiers with a leading upper-case letter on each component word, for example,

```
while Count > N do begin
   DoThis;
   DoThat;
   DoTheOther
end
```

This method also has merit. The upper-case leading letters serve as break marks, and there is no special problem with lengthy identifiers. However this method brings in two other issues for which a solution is hard to find. First, what should we do with the keywords when boldface is not available? Keeping the keywords in lower case, as before, makes it hard to distinguish the keywords from the identifiers. Thus the discrimination that I believe is important to readability is lost. Second, the identifiers begin to read like normal English prose. I am not sure this is correct. Although we want readable programs, to make them look like English prose may be a mistake.

This problem becomes more severe when a proportional typeface is used for writing programs. Proportional typefaces are quite common in textbooks and high resolution terminals. Often the proportional spacing is used in conjunction with boldfaced keywords. This gives something like

```
while (X > Y) do
   DoThis;
   DoThat;
   DoTheOther
end
```

Proportional spacing is a bane to the good alignment of programs. It is virtually impossible to do anything sensible with constructs like

```
procedure PUSH ({putting} NEWSYM:   SYMBOL;
                {onto}     SYMSTACK: STACK);
```

or

```
record
   Piece:    PieceType;
   Position: Square;
   Color:    PieceColor
end
```

Try keeping this alignment with proportional spacing and you get something like

```
procedure PUSH ({putting} NEWSYM:   SYMBOL;
                {onto}     SYMSTACK: STACK);
```

or

```
record
   Piece:    PieceType;
   Position: Square;
   Color:    PieceColor
end
```

A good programmer can use all kinds of subtle alignment conventions that are effectively ruled out with proportional spacing. Moreover, proportional spacing gives a program a truly prose-like look. Computer programs may not be mathematics or numeric tables, but to make them look like prose seems to be the wrong track.

The Up Arrow or At Sign

Pascal makes three different uses of the up arrow (↑). When the up arrow is not available (it certainly is not on most typewriters), the at sign (@) can be used in its place.

One use of this symbol is in a declaration specifying a pointer to an object of a given type, for example,

```
type
    TREE = ↑NODE;
    NODE =
        record
            ITEM:         VALUE_INFO;
            LEFTBRANCH:   TREE;
            RIGHTBRANCH:  TREE
        end;

var
    T:   TREE;
```

This use of the up arrow is quite natural; it suggests, for example, that a TREE is a pointer to a node.

The second use of the up arrow is for dereferencing a variable with a pointer type to obtain the value to which the variable points, for example, the reference

```
T↑.ITEM
```

I find this use of the up arrow a bit confusing. Whereas in a type declaration the up arrow reads "points to", when referencing a pointer value, the up arrow reads "value pointed to". There are various solutions to this problem. One would be to use a down arrow to indicate dereferencing, but this character is even more rare. Another solution, the one adopted in Ada, is to allow implicit dereferencing of one level and thus writing the preceding reference as

```
T.ITEM
```

Yet another solution would be to use a different character altogether to indicate dereferencing, although a good choice for this is not obvious.

The third use of the up arrow comes when the "buffer variable" associated with a file is denoted. For example if F denotes a file variable, then

```
F↑
```

denotes the current component of the file. This use of the up arrow seems unfortunate because in no way is there a suggestion of a linked structure usually associated with pointers or dereferencing.

All in all, I guess the at sign, a common symbol, is probably best. I have a clear preference for character sets that match standard typing and typesetting equipment.

Semicolons

In Pascal semicolons are particularly problematic. The issue is complicated by the use of "empty" statements and the use of begins and ends. Let's start with semicolons.

In the original spirit of Pascal, the semicolon was viewed as a "separator" and not a "terminator". Thus, for example, the semicolon was viewed much like a comma in a list. That is, if we have a list of three items,

```
X,Y,Z
```

we have two commas. Similarly, if we had a sequence of three statements, there would be two semicolons. Thus a statement never comes with its own semicolon. It is in this sense that we say

```
X := Y + 1
```

is a statement. Any semicolon that might appear afterwards is a result of it being in a sequence.

With a "terminator" view, a semicolon is much like the period at the end of an English sentence. That is, if we have three sentences, we have three periods. It is possible to apply this view to Pascal sometimes, but not always. For example, we can write

```
begin
    X := 1;
    Y := 1;
    Z := 1;
end
```

This is perfectly valid Pascal. However, in a strict sense this is not a sequence of three statements. It is a sequence of four statements in which the last statement is an empty statement. This is not a very pleasant way to think about the example and many programmers prefer to write this sequence without the last semicolon. This is my preferred view as well.

In some instances one cannot have a semicolon. For example, consider the following sequence:

```
begin
   WRITE ('This');          { -- semicolon required }
   if X > Y then
      WRITE ('That')        { -- no semicolon allowed }
   else
      WRITE ('the Other') { -- optional semicolon }
end
```

Here we must be aware of where semicolons can go and where they cannot go.
   Next consider the following three examples:

```
begin
   TEMP := X;
   X := Y;
   Y := TEMP;               { -- empty statement }
end
```

```
case I of
   1: DOTHIS;
   2: DOTHAT;
   3: DOTHEOTHER;           { -- no empty statement }
end
```

```
record
   A: REAL;
   B: REAL;
   C: REAL;                 { -- no empty field }
end
```

In the first example there is an implied empty statement, but in the second there is not. In fact, for the case statement the original definition of Pascal did not allow a semicolon. The new Pascal standard has been a bit more generous on the placement of semicolons and in fact the preceding case statement is now perfectly legal. The same applies to the record structure in the third example. There is no implied empty field list.

   This entire problem is compounded by the inconsistent use of bracketing for control structures. From this view the ideal structure is the *repeat* statement,

```
repeat
   DOTHIS;
   DOTHAT
until N > NUMITEMS
```

That is, the sequence is perfectly bracketed and any contained statements need only be indented one level. This clear bracketing structure can be extended to while and for statements with compound bodies, as in

```
while Z > Y do begin
    DOTHIS;
    DOTHAT;
    DOTHEOTHER
end
```

This pleasant way of displaying Pascal programs breaks down in other contexts. For example, consider

```
case I of
    1: DOTHIS;
    2: begin
          DOTHAT;
          DOTHATAGAIN
       end;
end

if X > Y then
    A := 1
else
    begin
      B := 1;
      C := 1
    end
```

Here the compound statements require two levels of indentation. Thus the pleasant symmetry of the *if-then-else* and *case* are lost by the most common case, that in which a statement is in fact a compound sequence of events.

The tangle of semicolons, empty statements, and compound statements requires much concentration in writing and reading a program. The attempt to gain natural symmetries is often lost, and inconsistent solutions to program layout are often adopted.

Pascal has some other minor anomalies. For example, it is not easy to understand whether subranges introduce a new type or not, and the syntax for record variants is awkward. In addition, the scope rules are quite complicated for a so-called small language.

Finally, let me not leave this chapter without taking good note of the many, many success in the design of Pascal. Although the language is many years old, it followed in the good tradition of Algol 60, cleared up many of its deficiencies, and introduced a number of new and creative ideas. It is these successes that have led in large part to the popularity of this language.

14

Is Pascal Too Large?

The widespread success of Pascal has been partly due to its perception as a "small" language. This, of course, is relative to other languages. We would be hard pressed to say with any rigor what a small language is. Pascal, perhaps, is thought of as small because of its economy of design and the attention given to eliminating language details that are unnecessary for most applications.

But Pascal is not as small as we think. It is more of a "moderate" size. For example, the definition of Standard Pascal itself requires about 100 pages of heavy prose—hardly indicative of a "small" language. Pascal is larger than the early versions of Basic or Lisp, and smaller than Ada or PL/I. Full Pascal implementations are not built in a month, nor is its implementation suitable to term projects in a graduate university course.

Pascal has evolved so widely and used in so many applications that extensions to the language have been common. Some of these extended versions have almost doubled the size of the original design. This has been caused partly by Pascal's lack of certain features, for example, string manipulation, parallel processing, exception handling, and separate compilation. This evolution has also been partly due to the fact that much more has been learned about languages since Pascal was conceived. Thus, with new vision to observe shortcomings in the Pascal language, we try to amend the original language through extended versions of it.

Virtually all implementations of Pascal, as well as the definitions of the standard version, were based on the original formulation of Pascal proposed by Niklaus Wirth [Wirth, 1971]. Here Wirth defined the design objectives for the language. There were two fundamental goals. The first was a language suitable for teaching programming. I take this to mean a language for a serious introductory course in programming using the best traditions of writing readable and well-structured programs. The second objective was to develop a language that could be efficiently and reliably implemented for the mainframe computers of the time. Typically a compiler for Pascal occupied 50,000 or 60,000 words of storage.

We return to these original two objectives, teaching and efficient implementation, to answer the question: Is Pascal too large? This is not an examination of application requirements that go beyond the initial bounds of Pascal, for instance, languages needed for systems programming, the writing of compilers, or programs for large interactive systems. We are only asking whether or not Pascal is too large for effective teaching and for efficient implementation.

By "teaching", I do *not* mean teaching computer science in general, for example,

    a. Teaching compiler writing
    b. Teaching advanced data structures
    c. Teaching operating systems

and so forth, but rather

- Teaching a serious introductory course in computer programming.

This limitation puts Pascal into a narrow focus. Obviously, if we extend teaching to mean "teaching computer science in general", the subject of this essay would be "Is Pascal Too Small", for it is indeed "too small" as a general-purpose language. Several proposed deletions mentioned later would never be suggested in this other context.

I believe the issue of a small teaching language is important. Students feel comfortable with a language they can learn completely. Implementations are less expensive, manuals and tutorials are smaller, and teaching itself is simplified.

Procedures as Parameters

The first feature that I would question in Pascal is rather large: parameters denoting procedures and functions. For instance, we may have

```
procedure GETAVERAGE (function F(X: REAL): REAL;
                      X1, X2: REAL;
                      INTERVAL: REAL;
                      {returns} var AVE: REAL);
```

Here F is a parameter that is a function.

To start with, this is a rather exotic feature of programming. It is useful in building mathematical libraries. In my years of teaching programming, including teaching Pascal to professional programmers, I have seldom seen the feature used. Of course, there are those who are familiar with the idea and who will argue vigorously for its inclusion in a language. But I believe quite strongly that, for teaching purposes, the case is just not there. Moreover, eliminating this from Pascal would certainly simplify its implementation.

Record Variants

The concept of a record variant is a useful idea itself, and cutting it from the language is a controversial proposal. The need for variants stems from data structures with alternative components. In Figure 14.1

```
record
    SYMBOL: SYMBOLID;
    LOCATION: INTEGER;
    case CLASS: CLASSIFICATION of
        SIMPLEID: (L: LENGTH)
        TYPEID: (T: TYPECLASS; PARAM: BOOLEAN);
        PROCID: (SCOPE: SCOPEREC;
                NUMPARAMS: INTEGER;
                TYPELIST: LISTSTRUCTURE);
        . . .
end
```

Figure **14.1**   *Record Variants*

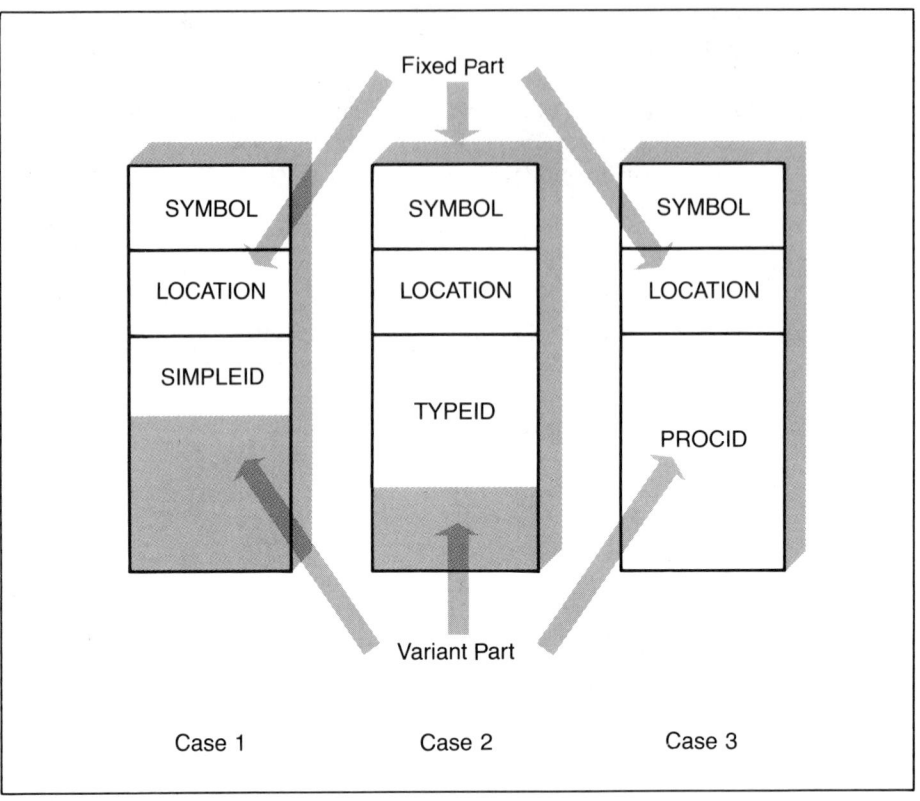

each alternative in the case part has different storage arrangements. Only one alternative will be present in a variant record value.

Such structures will always be an issue in programming as we build larger and larger systems. I acknowledge that records with alternative structures are a logically sound data type. However, record variants in Pascal introduce a definite complexity to the language for both student and implementor. There is even an option in the Pascal facility where no explicit tag field is given. This is truly an advanced feature in programming and hardly seems to fit a language for teaching.

My understanding is that record variants were included in Pascal to facilitate writing a Pascal compiler in Pascal itself. It is useful, even necessary, in systems applications. Large and sensible savings in storage can be achieved. But for the goals of the language, record variants, especially untagged variants, serve advanced purposes and could be eliminated.

Packed Structures

Economy of storage in Pascal can be expressed by the use of *packed* structures. This allows a user to designate an array or a record to be "packed", for instance,

```
var
     HEADER: packed array[1..72] of CHAR;
```

This means the compiler is informed that economy of storage is the main interest in reserving space for variables of a given type. For a packed array of characters, the classic case, this means that one character is allocated to each byte, rather than to each word, of storage. The result is that the compiler takes whatever steps are necessary to ensure that storage is economized even if access speed to components is sacrificed (see Figure 14.2).

The standard definition of Pascal leaves it to the implementation whether anything special should be done when a structure is packed. But the writer of a Pascal program must be aware of this packed issue. Strings must be defined as packed arrays of characters, and packed variables have special requirements for their use.

Sometimes packed structures are not compatible with unpacked structures of the same type. For instance, a component of a packed structure may not be an argument that corresponds to a variable parameter. This is a requirement for the compiler. The programmer must be aware of it as a linguistic feature. With the declaration,

```
procedure MAKELOWERCASE (var C: CHAR);
```

for instance, the call

```
MAKELOWERCASE (HEADER[I])
```

is not allowed. If Pascal is to be a teaching language, the kind of complexity introduced by packed structures is no recommendation.

The Goto

Pascal has a rich set of one-in, one-out control structures: the conditional statement, the case statement, while loops, repeat loops, and for loops. Pascal also has a modest facility for labels and *goto* statements—and this adds to the complexity of the language. In a curious way, Pascal requires that a label must be a sequence of digits and must be declared, so that the use of labels and goto's become uncomfortable—which is perfectly all right.

Figure 14.2   *Packed Data Structures*

Packed Data Structures

Using 32-bit words, 8 bits per character:

V	A	N	I
L	L	A	

Packed Data

V			

A			

N			

I			

L			

L			

A			

Unpacked Data

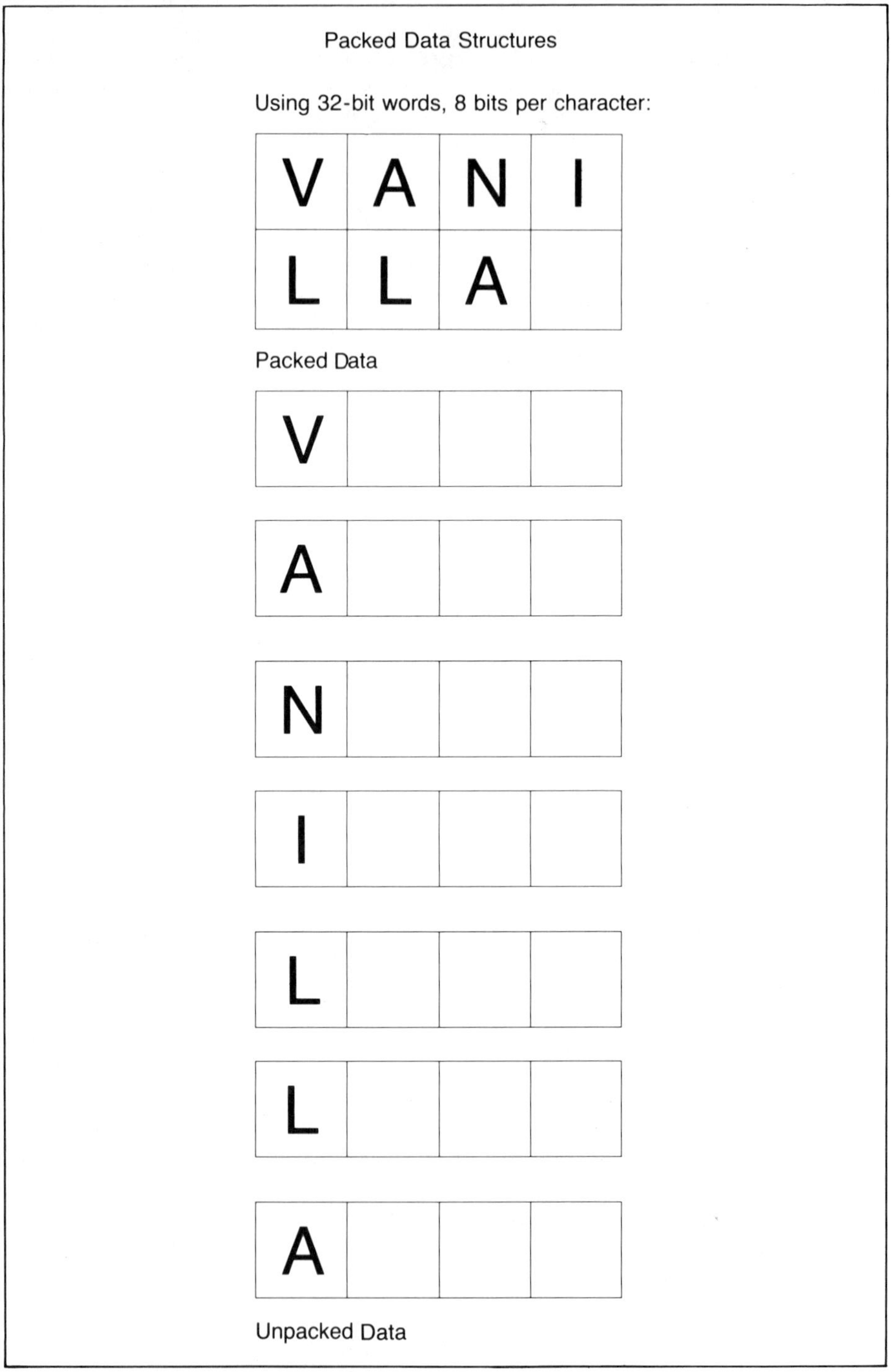

I say this because over the years there has been a great deal of attention toward supressing goto's. If Pascal is designed in such a way that goto's are, indeed, unwieldy and uncomfortable, why have the óption in the language at all? One of the best achievements in programming is the one-in, one-out control structures; the goto is fading away. In Pascal, the goto is a rarely used feature—and even when it is used, its value is questionable. This feature can be cut from the language.

Set Types

I do not wish to imply that set types are not useful. But the use of sets requires a measure of sophistication on the part of the programmer. It may be only a matter of training, but it takes time to be able to think of a set as a data type because the use of set types is not common.

Set types add complexity to Pascal. We must define when two sets are compatible and the rules in Pascal must be followed when making this definition. Moreover, the use of arithmetic operators (+, -, *) must be extended in order to define operations over sets. For example, + denotes set union and the relational operations are extended to denote set equality and set inclusion. Given the desire for simplicity in the language, are set types worthy of their inclusion?

There is one feature associated with set types that I would retain—the use of the operator *in* to denote whether a particular object is in a given collection of objects. Examples like

```
if NEXTCHAR in ['a' .. 'z'] then ...

if SYMBOL in [';', ':', ','] then ...

if OPTION in [NEWCHAPTER, NEWSECTION, NEWPAGE,
              NEWPARAGRAPH, NEWTABLE] then ...
```

are particularly useful when dealing with enumeration or character types. Retaining this feature does not mean keeping the facility for set types. The operator *in* can be included as part of the basic facility for ordinal types. We can then test whether a given value is in a particular collection of explicit values.

Procedures Nested Within Procedures

(*Note:* This topic and the next were discussed earlier in other settings.)

Nesting allows us to write procedures and to introduce pertinent names and definitions within the procedure itself. A name and its definition are considered local to the procedure and different from any use of the name outside the procedure. This fundamental idea has been a useful one in all programming languages that support it. Nesting helps us write procedures with a clear abstraction. The parameters of the procedures specify its public interface. Local information, pertinent only to the procedure, can be defined within the procedure and hidden from outside. The idea leads to both clarity and to efficiency.

In Pascal, a program consists of

- A sequence of label, constant, type, and variable declarations, followed by
- A sequence of procedure and function declarations, and then
- The body of the main program.

Procedures and functions can themselves have their own declarative parts which, in turn, can introduce new and nested procedures. It is this inner nesting of procedures within procedures that I wish to examine.

Consider the following program sketch:

```
program TEXTFORMATTER (INFILE, OUTFILE);
    -- declarations

    procedure GETFILE (parameters);

        . . .

        procedure GETLINE (parameters);
            . . .
        end; {GETLINE}


        . . .
        -- calls to GETLINE
        . . .
    end; {GETFILE}

begin
    -- statements of main program
end.
```

This program defines a procedure GETLINE that is called in the procedure GETFILE. GETLINE is nested within GETFILE.

Consider the following alternative rendering of the same program:

```
program TEXTFORMATTER (INFILE, OUTFILE);
    -- declarations

    procedure GETLINE (parameters);

        . . .

    end; {GETLINE}
```

```
procedure GETFILE (parameters);
    ...
    -- calls to GETLINE
    ...
end; {GETFILE}

begin
    -- statements of main program
end.
```

Now the procedure GETLINE is declared before the procedure GETFILE.

A procedure is, in a sense, a "constant". We do not change the definition of a procedure between calls (except indirectly by changing the values of global variables). The constant nature of procedures puts them in the same category as constants and types.

Procedures themselves are "large" items, and nesting them gets cumbersome. In fact, the nesting of procedures within other procedures is quite tedious to print in any reasonable way. The nested procedure must appear before the body of the host procedure. This nesting is really more distracting than helpful. As for implementing abstract data types, the lack of an "export" feature makes a solution via nesting unwieldy.

Declaring all the procedures at the outer level, on the other hand, has a certain advantage. The program structure itself takes the form of a simple linear listing of complete procedures. We can still group related procedures together in a program listing while keeping the linear arrangement.

Eliminating nested procedures would not especially simplify the definition or implementation of Pascal, but it would certainly simplify the syntax of programs. I think this cut would also make the structure of Pascal simpler for teaching, easier to explain, and more logical to use.

Unnamed Types

The familiar declaration

```
A: array[1..10] of INTEGER;
```

brings up a rule of good programming practice. The variable A is declared to have a given type, but the type is not named. Another unnamed type appears in the following:

```
R:  record
        X: REAL;
        Y: REAL;
        Z: REAL
    end
```

Even in

```
type
   BOOKINFO = array[1..MAXNUMPAGES] of
                  record
                     NUMLINES: INTEGER;
                     HEADER:   HEADERINFO;
                     ARTWORK:  BOOLEAN
                  end
```

we have a type named BOOKINFO, which is declared to be an array of records, but the record type itself is not named. I consider this another example of an unnamed type.

The problem with unnamed types is that type names should convey certain semantic information, even if used only for one variable. The preceding example can be better rendered as

```
type
   PAGEINFO =
     record
       NUMLINES: INTEGER;
       HEADER:   HEADERINFO;
       ARTWORK:  BOOLEAN
     end;
   BOOKINFO = array[1..MAXNUMPAGES] of PAGEINFO;
```

Here we see a symmetry between PAGEINFO and BOOKINFO, and the types are introduced one at a time.

Normally, a programmer will mix unnamed and named types:

```
type
   LINEMODE = (TEXT, EQUATION, TITLE);
   HEADERINFO =
       record
          POSITION: (LEFT, CENTER, RIGHT);
          CONTENT:  array[1..HEADERSIZE] of CHAR
       end;
var
   LINE,
   PREVLINE:  array[1..LINESIZE] of CHAR;
   LINESTATUS:  LINEMODE;

   BOOKDATA:
       array[1..MAXNUMPAGES] of
          record
             NUMLINES: INTEGER;
```

```
            HEADER:   HEADERINFO;
            ARTWORK:  BOOLEAN
         end;

     INFILE,
     OUTFILE: TEXT;
```

Here some of the types declared for the variable are given explicitly rather than named in a type declaration.

There are several problems with this example. First, Pascal requires that parameters be identified by the type name, rather than by giving the definition of the type. This rule guarantees type compatibility in a simple way. It also forces the programmer to name many of the types in a program.

But not all variables are passed as arguments to procedures and we can often still get by with the example declarations given earlier. In fact there is a tendency to use such declarations just because it's shorter to give the type in place than go to the trouble of giving it a name and its own type definition.

In the previous sample declarations, we must deduce exactly what these type definitions mean. Now consider the following rendering:

```
type
    LINEMODE       = (TEXT, EQUATION, HEADING);
    HEADERPOSITION = (LEFT, CENTER, RIGHT);

    LINETEXT       = array[1..LINESIZE] of CHAR;
    HEADERTEXT     = array[1..HEADERSIZE] of CHAR;

    HEADERINFO =
        record
           POSITION: HEADERPOSITION;
           CONTENT:  HEADERTEXT
        end;

    PAGEINFO =
        record
           NUMLINES: INTEGER;
           HEADER:   HEADERINFO;
           ARTWORK:  BOOLEAN
        end;

    BOOKINFO = array[1..MAXNUMPAGES] of PAGEINFO;

var
    LINE,
    PREVLINE: LINETEXT;
    LINESTATUS: LINEMODE;
```

```
BOOKDATA: BOOKINFO;

INFILE,
OUTFILE: TEXT;
```

Here a single convention is followed: every type definition is given a type name identifying its purpose. This leads to simpler and clearer definitions.

With this in mind, I suggest another cut to Pascal: elimination of unnamed types. This would certainly make the definition of Pascal easier and, I believe, would promote higher quality programs.

Conclusion

Pascal could well be shortened in these areas:

1. Parameters denoting procedures or functions
2. Variant parts of record structures
3. Packed structures
4. Labels and goto statements
5. Set types
6. Nested procedures and functions
7. Unnamed types

By so doing, we would actually enhance the original design objectives. There are other minor ways to shorten the language, such as eliminating the "downto" option in for loops and the predefined function DISPOSE. But the point is: Given the design objectives, we should take smallness of scale seriously.

Part Three

Putting It Together

15

An Annotated Example

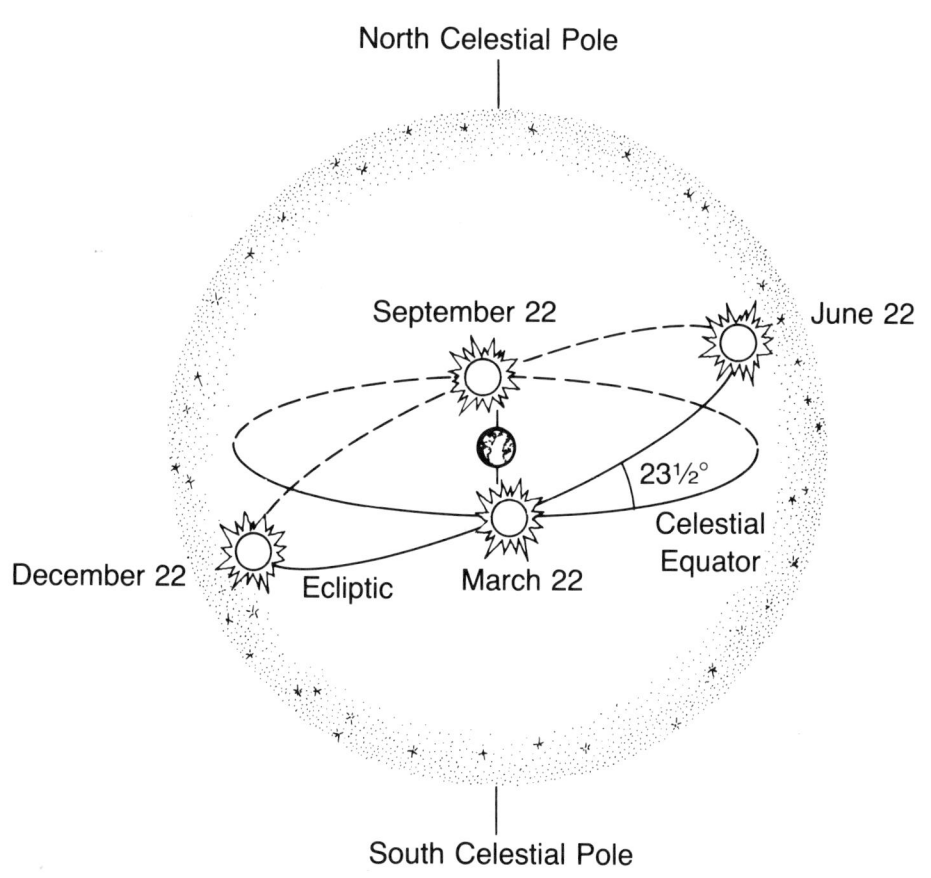

North Celestial Pole

September 22

June 22

23½°

Celestial
Equator

December 22

Ecliptic

March 22

South Celestial Pole

The writing of programs of professional quality is a complicated matter. It is both exciting and full of traps. This chapter presents a sample program that, by and large, incorporates the ideas mentioned in this work. Obviously any such example must take in account the limitations imposed by a single chapter in the book. The example, although not trivial, is little more than a toy as professional software goes. Professional software is usually far more complex and most often magnitudes larger. Nevertheless, this example is enough to be at least suggestive of what a professional program in Standard Pascal should look like.

The Problem—Text Formatting

The problem that we address is one from conventional text processing. This is the reorganization of a stream of text into a conventional page layout. This involves filling lines so that the lines are more or less balanced on the right, keeping margins, printing headers and page numbers, and a few of the special features usually required in these applications.

The kind of problem is suggested in Figure 15.1. In a simple word-processing system, for example, the user enters both text and controls; the latter govern the appearance of the text. The text may contain a control specifying that the following lines ought to be indented an additional ten spaces from the left margin. The system takes note of this control and, in printing the copy, appropriately indents the designated lines. Similarly, in a "what you see is what you get" editor, the image on the screen is not precisely that which is stored inside the memory of the computer. The computer's copy contains not only the text but additional controls. So, at the root of any of these systems is a file that contains not only the text that the user has entered, but also additional commands or controls for governing its layout.

The problem that we will synthesize from these applications is sketched in Figure 15.2. Here we assume that the input to our program is a file. The file contains text as well as control lines. The control lines govern the layout. Each control line begins with an at sign (@) and is followed by a single command. The output of the program is a file that is an image of a printed copy, suitably paged and organized. In giving this program we make some arbitrary assumptions about the kind of program that is desired and the environment for which is written. These assumptions are necessarily contrived to fit our purposes here.

Several kinds of commands can be inserted in the text of the document. These are:

SINGLESPACE	Print following text single-spaced (the default).
DOUBLESPACE	Print following text double-spaced.
HEADER "*string*"	Use *string* as a page header, left-justified.
PARAGRAPH	Print following text in paragraph style.
VERBATIM	Print following text exactly as it is given.

Figure 15.1   *Text Processing*

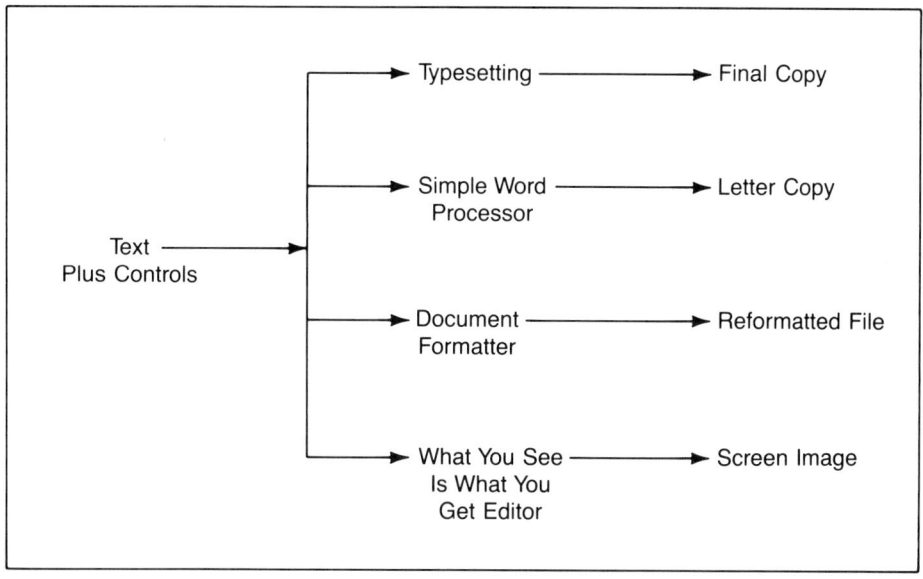

Figure 15.2   *The Problem*

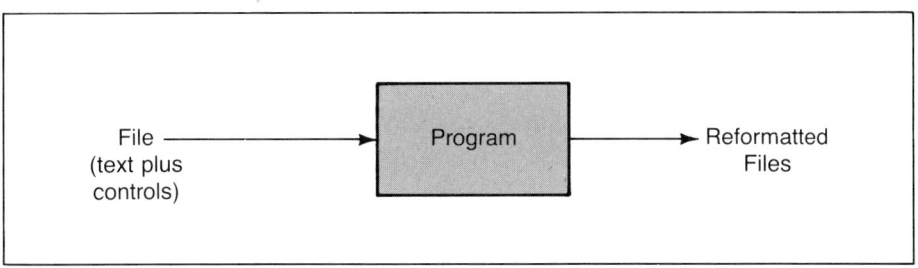

```
CENTER                      Center the following lines.
PAGE                        Start a new page.
INDENT n                    Indent following lines by n spaces.
NOSPLIT n                   Print following n lines as a unit, with no page break.
```

For example, the command

```
@INDENT 10
```

specifies that the subsequent text is to be indented 10 spaces from the left margin. I do not wish to elaborate more on the problem itself. The following program should state what is necessary to understand the problem in some detail.

(*Important Note:* The example of this chapter is seriously limited and secondary to our larger goal, a model program. In particular, we consider only a *minimal* text processing facility and what is needed in a minimal system. Your favorite feature is surely missing. On the other hand, the example demonstrates how useful an apparently simple, but well-crafted, small user interface can be.)

The Program

The design of the program is straightforward. Control lines are handled as they appear. For text lines, the program operates in one of several modes:

- Paragraph mode: The processing of lines of a paragraph.
- Verbatim mode: The processing of verbatim lines.
- Centered mode: The processing of lines that are to be centered.

The general operation can be defined as follows:

The current line is examined to see if the line is a control line or a line of text. If it is a control line, it is handled; otherwise, one of three subroutines is called:

- One will process paragraph lines until a line is reached that is a control line.

- A second will process verbatim lines until a control line is reached.

- The third will process centered lines until, again, a control line is reached.

Operation continues in this mode (for example, processing paragraph lines) until a control line is again encountered.

This design is summarized by the sketch of Figure 15.3. We see that control lines are processed one by one, then a group of text lines will be processed. These lines will be either paragraph lines, verbatim lines, or centered lines. A rough sketch of the algorithm corresponding to Figure 15.3 is as follows:

```
INDENTATION := 0;
MODE := PARAGRAPHSTYLE;
STARTDOCUMENT (OUTFILE, PAGE);

while MOREDATA(INFILE) do begin

    if NEXTCHAR(INFILE) = CONTROLCHAR then
        DOCOMMANDLINE ({updating} MODE, INDENTATION,
                                   INFILE, OUTFILE, PAGE)

    else if MODE = PARAGRAPHSTYLE then
        FORMATPARAGRAPHS ({using}    INDENTATION,
                           {updating} INFILE, OUTFILE, PAGE)

    else if MODE = VERBATIMSTYLE then
        COPYVERBATIM ({using}    INDENTATION,
                       {updating} INFILE, OUTFILE, PAGE)

    else { -- MODE = CENTERED }
        CENTERLINES ({using} INDENTATION,
                      {updating} INFILE, OUTFILE, PAGE)
end;
FINISHDOCUMENT (OUTFILE, PAGE)
```

This version of the algorithm indicates that some additional variables are needed to specify the actions completely.

It is instructive to consider how we would organize the program into independent packages (i.e., collections of related routines) that could be developed separately. This is part of the overall design.

In particular, the program is broadly organized as follows:

1. A main program and support routines which handle the commands and the formatting of individual lines of text.

2. A package of Input routines which provide the interface for getting and testing of lines of text from the input file.

3. A package of Control Line routines which handle the parsing of control lines.

4. A package of Page Layout routines which control the printing of pages in the desired format.

Figure 15.3   *The Overall Design*

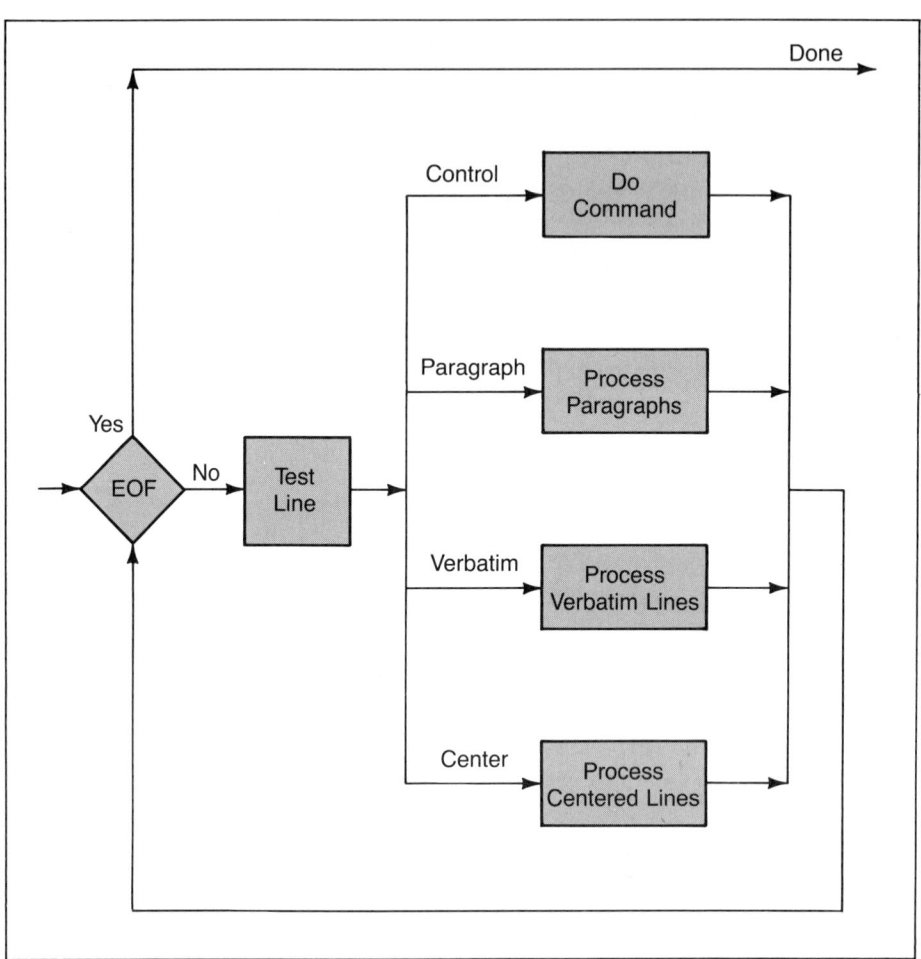

The packages may be viewed as underlying support for the main program. A sketch of the decomposition is given in Figure 15.4. The types associated with the parameters of the routines are given in the program itself.

This brief introduction to the problem and the program should be sufficient to understand the program itself. This is given in the appendix. Remember, our goal here is basically to show a program of sufficient quality that it can be read on its own.

Figure 15.4 *Decomposition of The Program*

```
{ ------------------------------------------------------------

  -- ** Input Routines

  -- function MOREDATA (var INFILE: TEXT): BOOLEAN;
  -- function NEXTCHAR (var INFILE: TEXT): CHAR;

  -- procedure GETLINE (var INFILE: TEXT; var LINE: LINEINFO);
  -- procedure GETWORD (var INFILE: TEXT; var WORD: LINEINFO); }


{ ------------------------------------------------------------

  -- ** Control line Routines

  -- function DIGITVALUE    (C: CHAR): INTEGER;
  -- function MAKEUPPERCASE (C: CHAR): CHAR;

  -- procedure PARSENUM (LINE: LINEINFO; STARTPOS: INTEGER;
                         var CMD: COMMANDINFO);
  -- procedure PARSEHEADER (LINE: LINEINFO; STARTPOS: INTEGER;
                           var CMD: COMMANDINFO);
  -- procedure PARSEARG (LINE: LINEINFO; BLANKPOS: INTEGER;
                        var CMD: COMMANDINFO);

  -- procedure PARSECONTROLLINE (LINE: LINEINFO;
                                var CMD: COMMANDINFO); }


{ ------------------------------------------------------------

  -- ** Page Layout Routines

  -- procedure STARTDOCUMENT  (var OUTFILE: TEXT; var PAGE: PAGEINFO);
  -- procedure FINISHDOCUMENT (var OUTFILE: TEXT: var PAGE: PAGEINFO);

  -- procedure NEWLINE (var OUTFILE: TEXT; var PAGE: PAGEINFO);
  -- procedure NEWPAGE (var OUTFILE: TEXT; var PAGE: PAGEINFO);

  -- procedure PRINTTEXTLINE  (var BUFFER: TEXTINFO;
                              var OUTFILE: TEXT; var PAGE: PAGEINFO);
  -- procedure PRINTERRORLINE (LINE: LINEINFO;
                              var OUTFILE: TEXT; var PAGE: PAGEINFO);

  -- procedure SETHEADER  (VALUE: TEXTSTR; LENGTH: INTEGER;
                          var PAGE: PAGEINFO);
  -- procedure SETNOSPLIT (NUMLINES: INTEGER;
                          var OUTFILE: TEXT; var PAGE: PAGEINFO);
  -- procedure SETSPACING (OPTION: SINGLEORDOUBLE; var PAGE: PAGEINFO); }
```

16

Conclusion

Mine is not the only voice offering a view of computer programming. This is not unusual. All the social sciences that have emerged in this century have had to endure the same travails in their evolution. We are in the same process. It will take us more time to learn what we teach every graduate student: discipline is not something we ought to do, discipline is something we must do.

But as a practical science, as a science of precision, we seem to be slow in passing through this evolution. I think this is because we attain a level of competence so quickly that we translate a "rush to knowledge" into a "rush to market." Once the finger is put to keyboard, the pressure is on. As academics, there is no end to our demands for rigor and precision. As professional programmers, there should be no end to our demand for excellence.

Of course, the problems are not easy, and the pressures to get the job done quickly are great. In identifying the varieties of P-sub-A programmers as a critical problem in the hierarchy of expertise is not to suggest that this is an exotic elaboration of the Peter Principle. One does not suddenly become static rising through the hierarchy. On the contrary, there is no doubt from my observations that many programmers who do not achieve that professional spark are simply weary or unwilling to do more battle with the unrealistic demands placed upon them. And, some do succeed. With appropriate personal qualities, they are a pleasure to work with.

The varieties of performance at work is not limited to our profession. Surely, one month's study at a local bank or insurance office could produce equally poignant examples. The issue is the same: the human element defines a profession.

The consideration of professional programming practice will eventually rebound to thinking about the human requirements for the user. At this very moment, I am waiting for a technology that will make the writing of programming books dramatically easier and less expensive, from first scruffy drafts to typeset copy. This is not an easy problem. It involves an extremely simple human interface, fast printers, legible copy, graphics, choice of fonts, monospaced program font with monospaced bold, integration with language compilers, portable terminals, and ease of secretarial help. Maybe the problem is with the software engineering teams, maybe it is with managers with tunnel vision, maybe it is too much to expect, or maybe no one thought out the problem that I must wrestle with today.

Two human identities are involved here. We human programmers endeavor to provide new tools for human users. They seek a better way to solve problems. Ours is no mean task. But it is not beyond our ability to think of lofty goals, for only in pursuit of them can we approach attaining them.

There are only a few masters in this dynamic, volatile profession. They face challenges that we cannot imagine and only they can meet. Our part is to survey our profession and choose the best ideas. If I have a fear, it is that our self-contentedness will undermine progress. If I have a hope, it is that craftsmanship and simplicity will become a dominant challenge.

The Annotated Program

```
{ -- ** Product Name:  TEXT.1
```
```
   -- ** Programmed by:  G. WASHINGTON
   -- ** Assisted by:    S. ADAMS, H. MARIE
```
```
   -- ** Date: October 1985


   -- ** Overview: The TEXT.1 document processing system allows the
   -- user to prepare a file of text with embedded control lines.
   -- Each control line contains a command. The commands specify how
   -- the pages of printed text will appear. The output is a new copy
   -- of the users original input text, suitably displayed and
   -- formatted. This document assumes a general (not detailed)
   -- understanding of the TEXT.1 User Manual.


   -- ** Resource Constraints: There are no particular constraints on
   -- this program as regards the amount of memory required for storage
   -- or the speed at which the program must execute.
```
```
   -- ** Input: A file of mode DOCUMENT. This file contains the text
   -- of a document and control lines.


   -- ** Output: A file of mode DOCUMENT, which can be directly sent
   -- to a line printer.

```
```
   -- ** Sample Input:


   --        TEXT.1 is the        basis of a preliminary text
   --        processing system with control lines. The system
   --        assumes that the text contains paragraphs which are
   --        to be displayed in conventional paragraph
   --        style.
   --        @INDENT 10
   --        The INDENT control line above specifies that the
   --        following text is to be indented 10 spaces from the
   --        left margin. This is what will be printed here.

   --        @INDENT 0
   --        @VERBATIM
   --        The VERBATIM control line prints        the lines
   --        exactly as they appear.
   --                 1
   --                  1
   --               1 2 1
   --              1 3 3 1
   --             1 4 6 4 1
```

Authors

I do not understand why more individuals and teams do not put their names on programs. The names of the authors are possibly the most important comments attached to a program. If any questions arise, problems occur, or modifications needed, a simple consultation with the authors may be indispensable. Even for classroom use, the name of the author is important. When someone has to evaluate a collection of programs, listing the author on the code can prevent some odd mistakes.

Date

The date of the program is certainly a useful piece of information. The problem is, which date shall one put? This is a tough call. Should it be the date at the time the comment itself is written? Should it be the date when the program is begun, or first submitted for compilation? Or execution? Should the history of the program be dated? Should the date give the actual date of the week, or just the month, or just the year? There is no universal answer to these questions. It depends on the circumstances. When a program is under development even the time of day may be important.

The date given here is that of a month and a year. This program is meant as an illustration of a certain kind of thinking about programming practice. The given date, shortly after the program was executed, indicates when the ideas mentioned in this book were fully crystalized in this example.

Prelude

The beginning of this program contains copious comments. This, of course, is a practice highly recommended here. The purpose of the prelude is not to decorate the program nor to give the reader verbiage. Its purpose is the enumeration of relevant facts.

In principle, the prelude to this particular program is enough to understand the entire program. In particular, it gives the overall purpose of the program, a sample of its input and output, an explanation of the commands that can occur in the text file, and a listing of any erroneous or unusual situations. The reader of the program need not refer to any other external documentation.

The idea of a self-documenting program is a good idea but not always possible in practice. As the specifications for a program grow, as special hardware is prescribed, special interfaces to an operating system, or complicated behaviors are needed, eventually the author must resort to external documentation. As much as possible, this should be kept to a minimum. When a program does require external documentation, the sources should be clearly cited so that the reader of the program knows exactly where to look.

Sample I/O

It is almost extraordinary how few programs contain examples of the input and corresponding output. It does not seem to matter if the programs are those of students in a introductory course or professional software engineers. We all learn by examples. Yet for computer programs, which must be read by other people, examples are extraordinarily rare.

Why is it so rare? My own guess is that there are several reasons. First, many programs are not written top-down and the final input-output behavior of the system is not clear until the very end. Thus it is almost impossible to write examples beforehand, and afterwards it is certainly a tedious task. Moreover, programmers may assume (often correctly) that any examples will be given in the supporting user documentation. It is also true that examples require a considerably investment of time if they are to be written carefully and included as part of the program documentation.

Examples, especially if done *before* coding, can "smoke out" the fuzzy designs can exist. To have to say what you mean by providing an exact replica of both the input and the output leaves no room for ambiguity. It forces the programmer to think ahead. The best case against examples rests on the difficulty of covering all the bases. Some programs might require thousands of examples to cover the various combinations and unusual cases.

The usefulness of examples to the program reader is beyond doubt. In one glance the behavior of the program is clear. Much less rhetoric is needed to explain general principles. Everyone gains. In short, more examples, please.

```
-- ** Sample Output:

--            TEXT.1 is the basis of a preliminary text
--         processing system with control lines. The system
--         assumes that the text contains paragraphs which are
--         to be displayed in conventional paragraph style.

--                    The INDENT control line above specifies
--                    that the following text is to be indented
--                    10 spaces from the left margin. This is
--                    what will be printed here.

--         The VERBATIM control line prints        the lines
--         exactly as they appear.
--                    1
--                   1 1
--                  1 2 1
--                 1 3 3 1
--                1 4 6 4 1
```

```
-- ** Layout Conventions:

-- * Vertical
-- LINES_PER_PAGE = 66
-- TOP_MARGIN     = 8 lines
-- BOTTOM_MARGIN  = 8 lines
-- TEXT_LENGTH    = 50 lines per page
-- MAX_NOSPLIT    = 50 lines
-- PAGE_NUM_LINE  = 6 lines from top of page

-- * Horizontal
-- CHARS_PER_LINE   = 85
-- LEFT_MARGIN      = 12 characters
-- RIGHT_MARGIN     = 10 characters
-- TEXT_WIDTH       = 63 characters per line
-- MAX_INDENT       = 50 characters
-- MAX_HEADER_WIDTH = 50 characters
```

```
-- ** Initial State of System:

-- PAGE_HEADER = none
-- MODE        = PARAGRAPH_STYLE
-- SPACING     = SINGLE
-- INDENTATION = 0
-- PAGE_NUM    = 1
-- LINE_NUM    = 1
```

Fine Print

The sample input-output here shows a few of the finer points in the program. A paragraph indent of five spaces is used if at least one space occurs at the left margin of a new paragraph. Otherwise, as in the indented text, no paragraph indent is used. Notice also that to return to the left margin, one must specify that the indentation is zero. Finally, the VERBATIM command leaves lines exactly as they are, even with obvious errors in the user's input. These are all nice to see illustrated.

Brevity

The purpose of a comment is to bridge the gap between the user's understanding of the problem and the program to solve the problem. As such, the page layout characteristics are specified somewhat like constant declarations. This format is not only relatively easy to read but suggestive of what follows. It is a terse and convenient way of establishing key information quickly.

The style of header comments in this program is somewhat "staccato." That is, there are numerous short sections, each describing some relevant piece of information. This kind of format is a good one, certainly preferably to long-winded paragraphs where the reader must delve carefully through the information. A careful balance must be struck between the niceties of normal English prose and the gibberish of the programming language world. Although the balance here may not be optimal (for instance, it might have been desirable to include a design diagram or examples of the unusual situations), the balance seems more or less satisfactory.

Startup

One of the confusing points about programs is exactly what assumptions are made when the system is started. In a large piece of software this problem can be extraordinarily difficult to express. Admittedly the program here is small, but its initial state is explicit.

```
-- ** Control Line Commands:

-- SINGLESPACE    The default. Specifies that all subsequent lines
-- are to be printed with single spacing.

-- DOUBLESPACE    Specifies that succeeding lines are to be printed
-- with double spacing. This applies to lines that are to be
-- centered, printed verbatim, and block items.

-- PARAGRAPH    Specifies that paragraph style is the mode of
-- printing. The first line of each paragraph is either flush left
-- (if no leading spaces are given on input) or is indented 5 spaces.
-- A paragraph is terminated by a blank line, a control line, or a
-- line with leading spaces. Once a paragraph is terminated, the next
-- line of text will be taken as the first line of a new paragraph.
--        The lines of the paragraph (except the last) are word-filled
-- so as to accommodate as many words as possible. The right margin
-- is ragged edged. An INDENT command specifies an indent for all
-- lines in the paragraph, thus shortening the standard line width.

-- VERBATIM    This command changes the style of printing to literal
-- (or verbatim) style. Lines are printed exactly as input. An INDENT
-- command causes a verbatim line to be shifted to the right but the
-- verbatim mode of output remains in effect until a PARAGRAPH
-- command is encountered.

-- CENTER    Specifies that the following lines are to be centered
-- between the current left margin and the right margin. If leading
-- spaces occur in the lines to be centered, they are counted as
-- characters in the lines to be centered. Trailing spaces, on the
-- other hand, are ignored.

-- PAGE    Specifies that subsequent text should be printed on a new
-- page, beginning on the first line.

-- HEADER "string"    This command specifies a header to be inserted
-- on subsequent pages. Normally this control line will appear at the
-- beginning of the document and affects all pages except the first
-- page, for which no header is printed. If this control line appears
-- after the first page is printed or after a previous control line
-- specifying a header, the newly specified header is used on
-- subsequent pages.
```

```
-- INDENT n    Causes a uniform indent of n spaces to be used for
-- all succeeding lines. An INDENT command can be used to establish
-- a new indent or, if n is zero, re-establish the indentation at
-- the left margin. The argument n must range from zero through 50
-- (barely enough room for even a single word). An indent command
-- affects verbatim lines as well as centered lines. For instance, if
-- an indent of 30 is called for and a CENTER command is later
-- encountered, the lines to be centered will appear midway between
-- the 30th character of a line of text and the right margin.

-- NOSPLIT n    Specifies that the succeeding n lines of text are
-- to be treated as a block and not broken over a page boundary. The
-- value of n can range from 1 (with no net effect) through 52 (a
-- very large block of unbroken text).
```

Errors

```
-- ** Errors:

--      The errors detected by TEXT.1 fall only in the syntactic
-- category.

--      1. Keyword Error. A line from the input file begins with an
--      at sign (i.e., presumably a control line) but is not
--      followed by one the command names.
--      2. Header Error. The argument given with a header command is
--      not a properly bracketed string (i.e., the initial or closing
--      double quotation mark is missing).
--      3. Argument Error. The argument for an INDENT or NOSPLIT
--      command is out of range.

--      Response: The line is printed as output and flagged with two
--      asterisks in the left margin.

-- ** Responses to Unusual Situations:

--      The philosophy of TEXT.1 is to be as generous as possible
-- when it comes to spurious combinations of input text and commands.
-- If at all possible, some reasonable action is taken. The
-- following situations are "unusual" and thus require special
-- definition.
```

```
--      1.  A control line appears within the range of a NOSPLIT
--      command.
--      Response: Process it as a control line, but do not count it
--      as a line of text for NOSPLIT.
```

The Unusual

```
--      2.  A piece of text extends beyond the right margin.
--      Response: Allow the line to extend beyond the right margin.
--      If it happens to extend even beyond the right edge of the
--      paper, excess text is printed on the next line.

--      3.  The input file is empty.
--      Response: One page is output, with an error diagnostic
--      printed on it.

--      4.  Text to be centered has leading spaces.
--      Response: Use the leading spaces as part of the text. Again,
--      a good choice is hard. The assumption here is the user wants
--      them (e.g., wants to move a header slightly off center). The
--      user can always delete the spaces.

--      5.  NOSPLIT is applied to paragraphed text.
--      Response: Treat as normal. This may mean that the argument
--      n given with NOSPLIT may not be exact, since line-filling
--      in paragraph mode can change the number of output lines.    }
```

Errors

Everyone likes to hear about what the program does when things go right. As a result, errors get short shrift. Although there are few possible errors in the text layout program, each are listed here. Listing them ensures that they are not only visible but also given full consideration by the programmer.

The Unusual

Life is not so simple that all events fall into "correct" category or the "error" category. From the user's point of view, the system can often give surprises. When things disappear from the screen, output overflows page boundaries, messages mean different things, or certain commands are not available, the user can quickly become confused. Often these behavior characteristics are left to chance. Nevertheless, the responses to unusual situations are important, so important that they are listed in the overall comments of this program.

```
program TEXT1 (INFILE, OUTFILE);

  const
    BLANK        = ' ';
    CONTROLCHAR  = '@';
    MAXLINEWIDTH = 120;
```

Visible Constants

```
    MAXINDENT      = 50;
    MAXHEADERWIDTH = 50;
    MAXNOSPLIT     = 52;

    { -- Vertical }
    LINESPERPAGE = 66;
    TOPMARGIN    =  8;
    BOTTOMMARGIN =  8;
    PAGENUMLINE  =  6;

    FIRSTTEXTLINE = 9;        { -- TOPMARGIN + 1 }
    LASTTEXTLINE  = 58;       { -- LINESPERPAGE - BOTTOMMARGIN }

    { -- Horizontal }
    CHARSPERLINE   = 85;
    LEFTMARGIN     = 12;
    RIGHTMARGIN    = 10;
    TEXTWIDTH      = 63;      { -- CHARSPERLINE - LEFTMARGIN - RIGHTMARGIN }
    MAXTEXTWIDTH   = 73;      { -- CHARSPERLINE - LEFTMARGIN }
    PARAINDENT     =  5;
    MAXBUFFERWIDTH = 182;     { -- MAXLINEWIDTH + LEFTMARGIN + MAXINDENT }

    STARTPRINTCOL = 13;       { -- LEFTMARGIN + 1 }
    ENDPRINTCOL   = 75;       { -- CHARSPERLINE - RIGHTMARGIN }

    NORMALMARGIN = '            ';
    ERRORMARGIN  = '**          ';

  type
    TEXTMODE      = (PARAGRAPHSTYLE, VERBATIMSTYLE, CENTERED);
    SINGLEORDOUBLE = (SINGLE, DOUBLE);
```

Naming Thicket

```
    COMMANDNAME = (SINGLESPACE, DOUBLESPACE, HEADER, NEXTPAGE,
                   PARAGRAPH,   VERBATIM,    CENTER,
                   INDENT,      NOSPLIT,     ERROR);
```

Visible Constants

The constants, MAXINDENT, MAXHEADERWIDTH, and MAXNOSPLIT, are used only within the procedure PARSEARG. In some sense, these constants are visible at the top level. The maximum indentation, for example, is hardly something that is invisible to the user. It could also be argued that the constants should be hidden within the the procedure itself. This "tension" is unresolved.

Naming Thicket

There is a very difficult naming problem here. The command for a new page is called PAGE. The program name for the record variable of type PAGEINFO is also called PAGE. In Pascal, the enumeration value for the command name cannot be identical to the record name. One of them had to budge. Since the enumeration value was only used twice, it was called NEXTPAGE.

```
TEXTSTR = packed array[1..MAXLINEWIDTH] of CHAR;
COMMANDINFO =
   record
      NAME:       COMMANDNAME;
      NUMERICARG: INTEGER;

      STRINGARG:  TEXTSTR;
      STRINGLEN:  INTEGER
   end;

TEXTIMAGE = packed array[1..MAXBUFFERWIDTH] of CHAR;
TEXTINFO =
   record
      WIDTH: 0..MAXBUFFERWIDTH;
      IMAGE: TEXTIMAGE
   end;

LINEIMAGE = packed array[1..MAXLINEWIDTH] of CHAR;
LINEINFO =
   record
      WIDTH: 0..MAXLINEWIDTH;
      IMAGE: LINEIMAGE
   end;

HEADERSTR  = packed array[1..MAXHEADERWIDTH] of CHAR;
HEADERINFO =
   record
      WIDTH: 0..MAXHEADERWIDTH;
      IMAGE: HEADERSTR
   end;

PAGEINFO =
   record
      LINENUM: INTEGER;
      PAGENUM: INTEGER;
      HEADER:  HEADERINFO;
      SPACING: SINGLEORDOUBLE
   end;

var
   INFILE, OUTFILE: TEXT;
   MODE:            TEXTMODE;
   INDENTATION:     INTEGER;
   PAGE:            PAGE;
```

Expansion

Global Variables

Expansion

The string argument is always a header, yet named generically as **STRINGARG**. This name is used with an eye toward expansion.

Global Variables

This program contains no global or "own" variables. This decision was deliberate.

However, the professional could well argue for two cases of own variables:

1. PAGE. This includes the four components of the page state: LINENUM, PAGENUM, HEADER, and SPACING. These could be made own to the page layout routines

2. INFILE and OUTFILE. INFILE would be own to the input routines. OUTFILE would be own to the page layout routines.

The rationale for making these variables own runs as follows:

- PAGENUM and LINENUM are not directly under the user's control (i.e., are hidden).

- The four components of the PAGE state are needed only in the layout routines.

- INFILE and OUTFILE would be protected from intrusion from other routines.

On the other side, my decision not to make them own runs as follows:

- The PAGE state variables are essentially visible to the user since they affect the printed copy (i.e., are not truly hidden). The commands themselves update the PAGE state.

- INFILE and OUTFILE are visible to the user.

More importantly, these effects must be understood in the main program.

There is another philosophy for using own variables. If a variable is visible in the main program, it is passed as a parameter to the relevant procedures. Once its value is obtained, its preservation is handled by the procedures that accepts its value. This seems to be a rational philosophy for avoiding global variables altogether while trespassing into the realm of own variables where necessary. These points will be taken up again.

```
{ -----------------------------------------------------------------------

   -- ** Input Routines

   -- function MOREDATA (var INFILE: TEXT): BOOLEAN;
   -- function NEXTCHAR (var INFILE: TEXT): CHAR;

   -- procedure GETLINE (var INFILE: TEXT; var LINE: LINEINFO);
   -- procedure GETWORD (var INFILE: TEXT; var WORD: LINEINFO);

   --------------------------------------------------------------------- }
```

```
function MOREDATA(var INFILE: TEXT):  {returns} BOOLEAN;
begin
   if EOF(INFILE) then
      MOREDATA := FALSE
   else
      MOREDATA := TRUE
end;
```

Renaming

```
function NEXTCHAR(var INFILE: TEXT): {returns} CHAR;

{ -- A slight trick is needed here to simulate an end of file or an
  -- end of line. }

   const
      NULLCHAR = CHR(0);

begin
   if EOF(INFILE) then
      NEXTCHAR := NULLCHAR
   else if EOLN(INFILE) then
      NEXTCHAR := NULLCHAR
   else
      NEXTCHAR := INFILE↑
end;
```

Tricks

Renaming

This function serves a simple renaming purpose. Rather than write

    if not EOF(INFILE) then ...

we write

    if MOREDATA(INFILE)

This call is made so frequently that it seems that the renaming idea is warranted on the grounds of readability.

Tricks

The function NEXTCHAR is used to peek at the next character in the input file and test it against a control character or a blank. A call to this function at the end of a file would abort the program. A call at the end of a line would give a blank (the wrong character). To avoid these spurious effects, a trick is used. In particular, the concept of a null character is invented and associated with zero. This allows the function NEXTCHAR to be used without further concern for these spurious effects.

A trick? Yes. Isn't this against the spirit of this work? Hmm.

```pascal
procedure GETLINE (({from} var INFILE: TEXT;
                    {into} var LINE:   LINEINFO);

{ -- This procedure obtains the next line of the input file and deletes
  -- any trailing blanks. }
```

One Purpose

```pascal
    var
       I: INTEGER;
       TRAILINGBLANKS: BOOLEAN;

begin
   I := 0;
   while not EOLN(INFILE) and (I < MAXLINEWIDTH) do begin
     I := I + 1;
     READ (INFILE, LINE.IMAGE[I]);
   end;
   READLN (INFILE);

   TRAILINGBLANKS := TRUE;
   while TRAILINGBLANKS and (I <> 0) do begin
     if LINE.IMAGE[I] = BLANK then
        I := I - 1
     else
        TRAILINGBLANKS := FALSE
   end;
   LINE.WIDTH := I
end;
```

Parameter Comments

```pascal
procedure GETWORD ({from}    var INFILE: TEXT;
                   {giving} var WORD:   LINEINFO);

{ -- This procedure extracts a word from the input file. }

    var
       I: INTEGER;
       BLANKCHAR: CHAR;

begin
   while (not EOLN(INFILE)) and (NEXTCHAR(INFILE) = BLANK) do
     READ (INFILE, BLANKCHAR);

   I := 0;
   while (not EOLN(INFILE)) and (NEXTCHAR(INFILE) <> BLANK) do begin
     I := I + 1;
     READ (INFILE, WORD.IMAGE[I])
   end;
   WORD.WIDTH := I
end;
```

One Purpose

A conscious attempt has been made to make each procedure one purpose. Not all the procedures are completely successful in this regard. This procedure, for example, not only obtains the next input line, but it also deletes its trailing blanks. This is a little bit more than one purpose. These are the kinds of things that programmers should keep under tight control.

Parameter Comments

Strategic comments like "from" and "to" are meant to serve a purpose. They attempt to itemize, in order,

1.   The inputs
2.   Updated variables
3.   The outputs

This scheme is used throughout the program. The parameters are always listed in this order. This promotes the view of procedures as mapping from inputs to outputs. They are only given in the procedure headers and not in the procedure calls. The reason for this is that such strategic comments may end up cluttering the program if used for all procedure calls. It seems that using them just for the procedure header is a good compromise.

```
{ -----------------------------------------------------------------

   -- ** Control line Routines

   -- function DIGITVALUE    (C: CHAR): INTEGER;
   -- function MAKEUPPERCASE (C: CHAR): CHAR;

   -- procedure PARSENUM      (LINE:     LINEINFO; STARTPOS: INTEGER;
                               var CMD:  COMMANDINFO);
   -- procedure PARSEHEADER   (LINE:     LINEINFO; STARTPOS: INTEGER;
                               var CMD:  COMMANDINFO);
   -- procedure PARSEARG      (LINE:     LINEINFO; BLANKPOS: INTEGER;
                               var CMD:  COMMANDINFO);
   -- procedure PARSECONTROLLINE (LINE: LINEINFO;
                                  var CMD: COMMANDINFO);



   --------------------------------------------------------------- }
```

```
function DIGITVALUE (C: CHAR): {returns} INTEGER;
begin
   DIGITVALUE := ORD(C) - ORD('0')
end;
```

```
function MAKEUPPERCASE (C: CHAR): {returns} CHAR;

{ -- Assumes continuous letter codes. }

begin
   if C in ['a'..'z'] then
      MAKEUPPERCASE := CHR(ORD('A') + (ORD(C) - ORD('a')))
   else
      MAKEUPPERCASE := C
end;
```

```
procedure PARSENUM ({using}  LINE:     LINEINFO;
                             STARTPOS: INTEGER;
                   {giving} var CMD:   COMMANDINFO);

{ -- This procedure analyzes the argument for a NOSPLIT or INDENT command.
  -- If the argument is not a well-formed number, CMD.NAME is set to ERROR.
  -- Otherwise the number is assigned to CMD.ARG. }

    var
       C: CHAR;
       VALUE: INTEGER;
       POSITION: INTEGER;

begin
    VALUE := 0;
    POSITION := STARTPOS;
    C := LINE.IMAGE[POSITION];

    while (C in ['0'..'9'])
    and (POSITION <= LINE.WIDTH) do begin
       VALUE := 10*VALUE + DIGITVALUE(C);
       POSITION := POSITION + 1;
       if POSITION <= LINE.WIDTH then
          C := LINE.IMAGE[POSITION]
    end;

    if POSITION = STARTPOS then
       begin
          CMD.NAME       := ERROR;
          CMD.NUMERICARG := 0
       end
    else
       CMD.NUMERICARG := VALUE
end;
```

Nesting

```
procedure PARSEHEADER ({using}  LINE:    LINEINFO;
                                STARTPOS: INTEGER;
                    {giving} var CMD:  COMMANDINFO);
```

Lowercase

```
{ -- This procedure analyzes the header for a HEADER command. If the
  -- header is invalid, CMD.NAME is set to ERROR. Otherwise the header
  -- is assigned to CMD.STRINGARG. }

  const
     QUOTEMARK = '"';
  var
     POSITION: INTEGER;
     LENGTH:   INTEGER;

begin
   if LINE.IMAGE[STARTPOS] = QUOTEMARK then begin
      POSITION := STARTPOS + 1;
      LENGTH := 0;

      while (LINE.IMAGE[POSITION] <> QUOTEMARK)
      and (POSITION < LINE.WIDTH) do begin
         LENGTH := LENGTH + 1;
         CMD.STRINGARG[LENGTH] := LINE.IMAGE[POSITION];
         POSITION := POSITION + 1
      end;
   end;
```

Naming

```
   if (LINE.IMAGE[STARTPOS] <> QUOTEMARK)
   or (LINE.IMAGE[POSITION] <> QUOTEMARK)
   then
      begin
         CMD.NAME := ERROR;
         CMD.STRINGLEN := 0
      end
   else
      CMD.STRINGLEN := LENGTH;
end;
```

Nesting

The procedures PARSENUM and PARSEHEADER are used only within the procedure PARSEARG. The procedure PARSEARG, in turn, is used only PARSECONTROLLINE. As such, these lower level procedures are candidates for nesting. That is, they could be declared within a procedure PARSECONTROLLINE. The non-use of nested procedures is something that is recommended here. As illustrated in this program, a simple linear listing of the procedures is quite satisfactory. Nesting them would, I believe, only confuse the issue.

Lowercase

Note that all comments are written in lower case, whereas programmer-defined names are upper case. The constant use of lower case for comments gives them another subtle isolation from the program body.

Naming

I must admit that this code underwent several revisions to get sufficient readability. The problem came in the distinction between the LENGTH, POSITION, and STARTPOS. I think the meaning is now clear, but it took work to get the names right.

```
procedure PARSEARG ({using}  LINE:      LINEINFO;
                              BLANKPOS:  INTEGER;
                    {giving} var CMD:    COMMANDINFO);

{ -- This procedure analyzes the argument for a HEADER, NOSPLIT, or
  -- or INDENT command. If the argument is missing or invalid,
  -- it sets CMD.NAME to ERROR. Otherwise it establishes the
  -- argument for CMD. }

  const
     MAXINDENT = 50;
     MAXHEADERWIDTH = 50;
     MAXNOSPLIT = 50;
  var
     POSITION: INTEGER;

begin
   POSITION := BLANKPOS;
   while (POSITION <= LINE.WIDTH)
   and (LINE.IMAGE[POSITION] = BLANK) do
       POSITION := POSITION + 1;

   if POSITION > LINE.WIDTH then {no arg found}
      CMD.NAME := ERROR
   else if CMD.NAME = HEADER then
      begin
         PARSEHEADER (LINE, POSITION, CMD);
         if CMD.STRINGLEN > MAXHEADERWIDTH then
            CMD.NAME := ERROR
      end
   else if CMD.NAME = NOSPLIT then
      begin
         PARSENUM (LINE, POSITION, CMD);
         if CMD.NUMERICARG > MAXNOSPLIT then
            CMD.NAME := ERROR
      end
   else if CMD.NAME = INDENT then
      begin
         PARSENUM (LINE, POSITION, CMD);
         if CMD.NUMERICARG > MAXINDENT then
            CMD.NAME := ERROR
      end
end;
```

```
procedure PARSECONTROLLINE ({using}  LINE: LINEINFO;
                            {giving} var CMD: COMMANDINFO);

{ -- This procedure analyzes a control line, and determines
  -- whether it is legal or not. If it is legal, the command
  -- name and its argument (if any) are established in CMD.
  -- If it is not legal, CMD.NAME is set to ERROR. }

   const
      MAXNAMELENGTH = 11;
   type
      CHARSTRING = packed array[1..MAXNAMELENGTH] of CHAR;
   var
      BLANKFOUND: BOOLEAN;
      BLANKPOS:   INTEGER;
      I, POSITION: INTEGER;
      NAMESTR:    CHARSTRING;

begin
   BLANKFOUND := FALSE;
   for I := 1 to MAXNAMELENGTH do begin
      POSITION := I + 1; { -- skip over @ sign }
      if (POSITION > LINE.WIDTH) or BLANKFOUND then
         NAMESTR[I] := BLANK
      else if LINE.IMAGE[POSITION] = BLANK then
         begin
            NAMESTR[I] := BLANK;
            BLANKFOUND := TRUE;
            BLANKPOS   := POSITION;
         end
      else
         NAMESTR[I] := MAKEUPPERCASE(LINE.IMAGE[POSITION])
   end;

   if NAMESTR = 'SINGLESPACE' then
      CMD.NAME := SINGLESPACE
   else if NAMESTR = 'DOUBLESPACE' then
      CMD.NAME := DOUBLESPACE
   else if NAMESTR = 'PARAGRAPH  ' then
      CMD.NAME := PARAGRAPH
   else if NAMESTR = 'VERBATIM   ' then
      CMD.NAME := VERBATIM
   else if NAMESTR = 'CENTER     ' then
      CMD.NAME := CENTER
   else if NAMESTR = 'PAGE       ' then
      CMD.NAME := NEXTPAGE
```

```
  else if NAMESTR = 'HEADER      ' then
     CMD.NAME := HEADER
  else if NAMESTR = 'INDENT      ' then
     CMD.NAME := INDENT
  else if NAMESTR = 'NOSPLIT     ' then
     CMD.NAME := NOSPLIT
  else
     CMD.NAME := ERROR;

  if CMD.NAME in [HEADER, NOSPLIT, INDENT] then
     PARSEARG (LINE, BLANKPOS, CMD)
end;
```

```
{ ----------------------------------------------------------------------
```
Own Variables
```
   -- ** Page Layout Routines

   -- procedure STARTDOCUMENT  (var OUTFILE: TEXT; var PAGE: PAGEINFO);
   -- procedure FINISHDOCUMENT (var OUTFILE: TEXT: var PAGE: PAGEINFO);

   -- procedure NEWLINE (var OUTFILE: TEXT; var PAGE: PAGEINFO);
   -- procedure NEWPAGE (var OUTFILE: TEXT; var PAGE: PAGEINFO);

   -- procedure PRINTTEXTLINE  (var BUFFER: TEXTINFO;
                                var OUTFILE: TEXT; var PAGE: PAGEINFO);
   -- procedure PRINTERRORLINE (LINE: LINEINFO;
                                var OUTFILE: TEXT; var PAGE: PAGEINFO);

   -- procedure SETHEADER  (VALUE: TEXTSTR; LENGTH: INTEGER;
                            var PAGE: PAGEINFO);
   -- procedure SETNOSPLIT (NUMLINES: INTEGER;
```
Odd Parameter
```
                            var OUTFILE: TEXT; var PAGE: PAGEINFO);
   -- procedure SETSPACING (OPTION: SINGLEORDOUBLE;
                            var PAGE: PAGEINFO);


   ------------------------------------------------------------------  }



procedure STARTDOCUMENT (var OUTFILE: TEXT; var PAGE: PAGEINFO);

{ -- This procedure establishes the protocols for the first page of output. }

   var
      I: INTEGER;

begin
   for I := 1 to (FIRSTTEXTLINE - 1) do
      WRITELN (OUTFILE);

   PAGE.PAGENUM := 1;
   PAGE.LINENUM := FIRSTTEXTLINE;

   for I := 1 to MAXHEADERWIDTH do
      PAGE.HEADER.IMAGE[I] := BLANK;
   PAGE.HEADER.WIDTH := 0;

   PAGE.SPACING := SINGLE
end;
```

```
procedure FINISHDOCUMENT ({updating} var OUTFILE: TEXT; var PAGE: PAGEINFO);

{ -- This procedure completes the last page of a document. If no lines have
  -- been printed (an empty INFILE), a message is printed. }

    var
        I, NUMBLANKLINES: INTEGER;

begin
    if (PAGE.PAGENUM = 1) and (PAGE.LINENUM = FIRSTTEXTLINE) then
        WRITE (OUTFILE, '** NO TEXT GIVEN AS INPUT.');
```

Simple Names

```
    NUMBLANKLINES := LINESPERPAGE - PAGE.LINENUM + 1;
    for I := 1 to NUMBLANKLINES do
        WRITELN (OUTFILE)
end;




procedure NEWPAGE ({updating} var OUTFILE: TEXT; var PAGE: PAGEINFO);

{ -- This procedure completes the current page and starts a new one,
  -- including a new page number and page header. }

    var
        I, NUMBLANKLINES: INTEGER;

begin
    NUMBLANKLINES := LINESPERPAGE - PAGE.LINENUM;
    for I := 1 to NUMBLANKLINES do
        WRITELN (OUTFILE);
```

Blank Lines

```
    PAGE.PAGENUM := PAGE.PAGENUM + 1;
    for I := 1 to (PAGENUMLINE - 1) do
        WRITELN (OUTFILE);
```

Localization

```
    WRITE (OUTFILE, NORMALMARGIN);
    WRITE (OUTFILE, PAGE.PAGENUM : 1);
    WRITE (OUTFILE, BLANK, BLANK);
    for I := 1 to PAGE.HEADER.WIDTH do
        WRITE (OUTFILE, PAGE.HEADER.IMAGE[I]);

    for I := PAGENUMLINE to FIRSTTEXTLINE do
        WRITELN(OUTFILE);
    PAGE.LINENUM := FIRSTTEXTLINE
end;
```

Own Variables

PAGE is a record with four components. These are

LINENUM   For preserving the current line number.
PAGENUM   For preserving the current page number.
HEADER   For preserving the current page header.
SPACING   A flag indicating single or double spacing.

These are candidates for the concept of hidden or own variables within this collection of routines. The page number and line number are not used or referenced outside the routines. Values for the page header HEADER and spacing option SPACING, on the other hand, are used (i.e., obtained) outside the package. If made own, when used outside, they should have explicit roles as arguments. It is only within the collection of routines that these variables should be own. Note that making PAGE own would simplify procedure calls.

The difference between global and own variables will always be a gray area. The goal in this program was to have absolutely no global variables nor any questionable own variables.

Odd Parameter

The procedures, SETHEADER, SETNOSPLIT, SETSPACING, form a convenient group for establishing values that are to be preserved. Unfortunately the symmetry is not perfect. SETHEADER and SETSPACING simply establish values, whereas SETNOSPLIT can actually modify the output file OUTFILE. In the case where a block of lines cannot fit on the current page, a new page is called for in the body of SETNOSPLIT.

Simple Names

Here the variable name I is used for a kind of generic counter. On the other hand, the variable NUMBLANKLINES is meant to be quite evocative. The reason for this is that it is all too easy to go overboard and try to give a detailed meaning for every name in the program. For simple counters, temporary values, subscripts, and so forth, an occasional lapse into one letter names seems wise. The key point is to make sure that the code is readable in its own right.

Blank Lines

Here is a clear example of the use of blank lines to separate conceptual units. The units are

Finish old page.
Start new page.
Print header.
Advance to first text line.

Localization

Line numbers and page numbers are maintained by the procedures NEWLINE and NEWPAGE. Other than setting their initial values, these two procedures are the only places where these variables are referenced.

```
procedure NEWLINE ({updating} var OUTFILE: TEXT; var PAGE: PAGEINFO);

{ -- This procedure causes an advance to a new line. }

begin
   if PAGE.LINENUM = LASTTEXTLINE then
      NEWPAGE (OUTFILE, PAGE)
   else
      begin
         WRITELN (OUTFILE);
         PAGE.LINENUM := PAGE.LINENUM + 1
      end;

   if PAGE.SPACING = DOUBLE then
      if PAGE.LINENUM = LASTTEXTLINE then
         NEWPAGE (OUTFILE, PAGE)
      else
         begin
            WRITELN (OUTFILE);
            PAGE.LINENUM := PAGE.LINENUM + 1
         end
end;
```

```
procedure PRINTTEXTLINE ({updating} var BUFFER:  TEXTINFO;
                                       var OUTFILE: TEXT;
                                       var PAGE:    PAGEINFO);

{ -- This procedure outputs a line of text for printing. If the line is
  -- too long, excess characters are printed in the right margin and
  -- continued on the following line, with no indent. }

   var
      I: INTEGER;

begin
   WRITE (OUTFILE, NORMALMARGIN);
   if BUFFER.WIDTH <= MAXTEXTWIDTH then
      for I := 1 to BUFFER.WIDTH do
         WRITE (OUTFILE, BUFFER.IMAGE[I])
   else
      begin
        for I := 1 to MAXTEXTWIDTH do
           WRITE (OUTFILE, BUFFER.IMAGE[I]);
        NEWLINE (OUTFILE, PAGE);
        WRITE (OUTFILE, NORMALMARGIN);
        for I := MAXTEXTWIDTH + 1 to BUFFER.WIDTH do
           WRITE (OUTFILE, BUFFER.IMAGE[I])
      end;
```

Side Effect?

```
   NEWLINE (OUTFILE, PAGE);
   BUFFER.WIDTH := 0
end;
```

```
procedure PRINTERRORLINE ({using} LINE: LINEINFO;
                          {updating} var OUTFILE: TEXT;
                                     var PAGE: PAGEINFO);

{ -- This procedure outputs an erroneous control line. }

    var
      I: INTEGER;

begin
  WRITE (OUTFILE, ERRORMARGIN);
  if LINE.WIDTH <= MAXTEXTWIDTH then
    for I := 1 to LINE.WIDTH do
      WRITE (OUTFILE, LINE.IMAGE[I])
  else
    begin
      for I := 1 to MAXTEXTWIDTH do
        WRITE (OUTFILE, LINE.IMAGE[I]);
      NEWLINE (OUTFILE, PAGE);
      WRITE (OUTFILE, NORMALMARGIN);
      for I := MAXTEXTWIDTH + 1 to LINE.WIDTH do
        WRITE (OUTFILE, LINE.IMAGE[I])
    end;
  NEWLINE (OUTFILE, PAGE)
end;
```

Multiple Commands

```
procedure SETHEADER ({using} VALUE:  TEXTSTR;
                             LENGTH: INTEGER;
                      {updating} var PAGE: PAGEINFO);

{ -- Establishes a new header for subsequent pages. }

    var
      I: INTEGER;

begin
  for I := 1 to LENGTH do
    PAGE.HEADER.IMAGE[I] := VALUE[I];
  PAGE.HEADER.WIDTH := LENGTH
end;
```

Header Comments

Side Effect?

There is a slight unpleasantry in this procedure. After printing the line of text in the text buffer, the buffer width set to zero. This is a kind of "second" purpose, or, if you will, a "side effect". There seems no easy way around this problem, although many programmers use these kinds of problems as excuses for complicated code.

Multiple Commands

One likely extension to this program is allowing multiple commands on a line, for instance,

```
@PARAGRAPH, INDENT 10
```

As a result, a careful naming distinction has been kept through the program.

Control line: A line beginning with @.
Command: A component of a control line.

If this distinction had not been kept and the extension were implemented, *serious* naming problems would arise.

Header Comments

Throughout the program a very brief English interpretation of the intent of the procedure is given. This is like a mini-specification of the procedure's operations. No particular attempt has been made to be detailed in the procedure header comments. Obviously more rigor is of more value, but not when it interferes and clutters the program text.

It could be argued that in short procedures like this, a header comment is not warranted. It is a bit tedious at times to give header comments for small procedures, but they still serve a good value and can be ignored by the programmer who wishes to.

```
procedure SETNOSPLIT ({using} NUMLINES: INTEGER;
                        {updating} var INFILE: TEXT;
                                    var PAGE: PAGEINFO);

{ -- This procedure checks that there are NUMLINES remaining
  -- on the current page. If not, a new page is established. }

   var
      BLOCKSIZE: INTEGER;

begin
   if (PAGE.SPACING = SINGLE) then
      BLOCKSIZE := NUMLINES
   else  { -- DOUBLE spacing }
      BLOCKSIZE := 2*NUMLINES - 1;
   if (PAGE.LINENUM + BLOCKSIZE - 1) > LASTTEXTLINE then
      NEWPAGE (OUTFILE, PAGE)
end;




procedure SETSPACING ({using} OPTION: SINGLEORDOUBLE;
                        {updating} var PAGE: PAGEINFO);

{ -- Sets indicator for SINGLE or DOUBLE spacing. }
 begin
   PAGE.SPACING := OPTION
end;
```

```
{ ----------------------------------------------------------------- }


{ -- ** Main Algorithms }


procedure ADDTEXT ({using} LINE: LINEINFO;
                   {to   } var BUFFER: TEXTINFO);

{ -- This procedure appends the text in LINE to the text buffer. }

    var
       I: INTEGER;

begin
    for I := 1 to LINE.WIDTH do
       BUFFER.IMAGE[BUFFER.WIDTH + I] := LINE.IMAGE[I];

    BUFFER.WIDTH := BUFFER.WIDTH + LINE.WIDTH
end;




procedure ADDSPACES ({using} NUMSPACES: INTEGER;
                     {updating} var BUFFER: TEXTINFO;

{ -- This procedure adds spaces to the text BUFFER. }

    var
       I: INTEGER;

begin
    for I := 1 to NUMSPACES do
       BUFFER.IMAGE[BUFFER.WIDTH + I] := BLANK;

    BUFFER.WIDTH := BUFFER.WIDTH + NUMSPACES
end;
```

```
procedure CENTERLINES ({using} INDENTATION: INTEGER;
                       {updating} var INFILE:  TEXT;
                                  var OUTFILE: TEXT;
                                  var PAGE:    PAGEINFO);

{ -- This procedure takes lines from the input file and centers
  -- them on the output file. Leading spaces on input lines are
  -- counted as text for centering. The indentation is used as
  -- the left margin for centering. }
```

Lineup

```
    var
        LINE:      LINEINFO;
        BUFFER:    TEXTINFO;
        PADDING:   INTEGER;
        PRINTWIDTH: INTEGER;
```

Naming Conventions

```
begin
    BUFFER.WIDTH := 0;
    while MOREDATA(INFILE)
    and (NEXTCHAR(INFILE) <> CONTROLCHAR) do begin
        GETLINE (INFILE, LINE);
        ADDSPACES (INDENTATION, BUFFER);

        PRINTWIDTH := TEXTWIDTH - INDENTATION;
        if LINE.WIDTH < PRINTWIDTH then
            begin
                PADDING := (PRINTWIDTH - LINE.WIDTH) div 2;
                ADDSPACES (PADDING, BUFFER)
            end;

        ADDTEXT (LINE, BUFFER);
        PRINTTEXTLINE (BUFFER, OUTFILE, PAGE)
    end

end;
```

Lineup

In the variable declarations given here, the type names of each variable are aligned. On the other hand, one could have written the variable declaration as follows:

```
LINE: LINEINFO;
BUFFER: TEXTINFO;
PADDING: INTEGER;
PRINTWIDTH: INTEGER;
```

One goal of alignment is to show symmetry among related concepts. Another is for easy look-up. The variables and their type names have no particular interrelationship. Hence, the alignment, while fine, is not critical. I have seen programmers go to extremes to line up virtually everything in a program, whether or not there is any semantic reason to do so. The strategy here is to do it when it counts, and perhaps a little more. This example truly gets down to the fine print.

Naming Convention

No name in this program underwent more revisions than the use of the suffix WIDTH. This suffix is used in many places, for example, in the name TEXTWIDTH and in the record component BUFFER.WIDTH. The basic problem ran like this. Lines generally are considered to have "length". Pages also have a "length". So there is the length of a line, the length of a page, the length of a header, the length of a word, and so forth. Always using the suffix LENGTH, as done initially, led to much confusion. The problem is that pages have two dimensions and treating them both as "lengths" was confusing. In the end, it was decided that virtually every name that referred to a horizontal dimension was specified by WIDTH.

There is another option that might also be satisfactory. That is, to avoid any use of the LENGTH attribute as regards the vertical dimension of the page, and reserve the word LENGTH only for the horizontal dimension. This, perhaps, would be more traditional and thus easier. It's a toss-up.

```
procedure COPYVERBATIM ({using} INDENTATION: INTEGER;
                       {updating}  var INFILE:  TEXT;
                                   var OUTFILE: TEXT;
                                   var PAGE:    PAGEINFO);

{ -- This procedure copies lines from the input file to the output file,
  -- adding the current indentation to each output line. }

    var
       LINE:   LINEINFO;
       BUFFER: TEXTINFO;
```

Reading Aloud

```
begin
    BUFFER.WIDTH := 0;
    while MOREDATA(INFILE)
    and (NEXTCHAR(INFILE) <> CONTROLCHAR) do begin
        GETLINE (INFILE, LINE);
        ADDSPACES (INDENTATION, BUFFER);
        ADDTEXT (LINE, BUFFER);
        PRINTTEXTLINE (BUFFER, OUTFILE, PAGE)
    end
end;
```

Reading Aloud

It may be instructive to show the effect of a good choice of names in making it easy to read a program aloud. Consider the following reading of the referenced algorithm.

> While there is more DATA in the INFILE
> and the next CHARACTER on the INFILE is a control character
> do the following:
>
> 1.   Get a LINE from the INFILE.
> 2.   Add the spaces of INDENTATION to the BUFFER.
> 3.   Add the text contained in LINE to the BUFFER
> 4.   Print the text line in BUFFER on the OUTFILE, updating the PAGE.

This kind of reading goes on in the programmer's mind as the code is written. The closer the code comes to easy reading, the easier the digestion; it's what naming is all about.

I do not want to imply that English should be used as a basis for language syntax. An inspiration, yes. But programs are basically like tables or equations. They need a terseness of their own, a rigor, and a punctuated format. Within this technical framework, a good English-like rendering should at least be possible. Compare the superiority of the above mentioned procedure with the following:

```
while not EOF(INFILE) and (INFILE↑ <> '@') do begin
   GETL(FILEIN, L);
   SPACES(INDENT, BUFF);
   TEXT (L, BUFF);
   PRINTL (BUFF, FILEOUT, PAGE)
end
```

It is possible, stretching the imagination, to give some reading aloud of this fragment. But it is a long stretch—testing of the human reader.

```
procedure PROCESSWORD ({using} INDENTATION: INTEGER;
                                WORD: LINEINFO;
                       {updating} var BUFFER: TEXTINFO;
                                var OUTFILE: TEXT;
                                var PAGE: PAGEINFO);

{ -- This procedure handles a single word. }
```

```
begin
    if (WORD.WIDTH + BUFFER.WIDTH) <= TEXTWIDTH then
        begin
            ADDTEXT (WORD, BUFFER);
            ADDSPACES (1, BUFFER)
        end
    else if (WORD.WIDTH + INDENTATION) <= TEXTWIDTH then
        begin
            PRINTTEXTLINE (BUFFER, OUTFILE, PAGE);
            ADDSPACES (INDENTATION, BUFFER);
            ADDTEXT (WORD, BUFFER);
            ADDSPACES (1, BUFFER)
        end
    else
        begin
            if BUFFER.WIDTH > INDENTATION then
                begin
                    PRINTTEXTLINE (BUFFER, OUTFILE, PAGE);
                    ADDSPACES (INDENTATION, BUFFER)
                end;
            ADDTEXT (WORD, BUFFER);
            PRINTTEXTLINE (BUFFER, OUTFILE, PAGE);
            ADDSPACES (INDENTATION, BUFFER)
        end
end;
```

Algorithm Comments

For some, the procedure given here may be confusing. It could well be argued that the algorithm itself needs particular comments. This could take the form of

- A sketch of the algorithm given in the procedure header comment
- Strategic comments within the body of the procedure

This has not been done here. This procedure and the next were revised just to achieve one goal—to make the algorithm so transparent as to not require such comments. The reader must judge the success.

```pascal
procedure FORMATPARAGRAPHS ({using} INDENTATION: INTEGER;
                           {updating} var INFILE:   TEXT;
                                      var OUTFILE: TEXT;
                                      var PAGE:    PAGEINFO);

{ -- This procedure reformats text into whole paragraphs. It keeps
  -- processing input lines until a control line is reached. }

  var
     LINE: LINEINFO;
     WORD: LINEINFO;
     BUFFER: TEXTINFO;

begin
  BUFFER.WIDTH := 0;
  ADDSPACES (INDENTATION, BUFFER);
  while MOREDATA(INFILE)
  and (NEXTCHAR(INFILE) <> CONTROLCHAR) do begin
    if EOLN(INFILE) then { -- an empty line }
```

Inline Comments

```pascal
      begin
        if BUFFER.WIDTH > INDENTATION then
          PRINTTEXTLINE (BUFFER, OUTFILE, PAGE);
        READLN (INFILE);
        NEWLINE (OUTFILE, PAGE);
        ADDSPACES (INDENTATION, BUFFER)
      end
    else
      begin
        if NEXTCHAR(INFILE) = BLANK then { -- new paragraph }
          begin
            if BUFFER.WIDTH > INDENTATION then
              PRINTTEXTLINE (BUFFER, OUTFILE, PAGE);
            ADDSPACES (INDENTATION + PARAINDENT, BUFFER)
          end;
```

Long Procedures

```pascal
        GETWORD (INFILE, WORD);
        while WORD.WIDTH <> 0 do begin
          PROCESSWORD (INDENTATION, WORD, BUFFER, OUTFILE, PAGE);
          GETWORD (INFILE, WORD)
        end;
        READLN(INFILE)
      end
  end;

  if BUFFER.WIDTH > INDENTATION then
    PRINTTEXTLINE (BUFFER, OUTFILE, PAGE)
end;
```

Inline Comments

Yes, I believe they are needed.

Long Procedures

Originally, GETWORD was not a procedure; its body was inline here. This was definitely too much for normal comprehension. It needed, in some way, to be revised. The normal recourse was taken to split the procedure into smaller procedures. This means searching for a fragment that could stand alone as a conceptual unit and packaged as a subprocedure. A decent slice of the cake was the fragment that became the body of GETWORD.

```
procedure DOCOMMANDLINE ({updating} var MODE:        TEXTMODE;
                                     var INDENTATION: INTEGER;
                                     var INFILE:      TEXT;
                                     var OUTFILE:     TEXT;
                                     var PAGE:        PAGEINFO);

{ -- This procedure extracts a control line from the input file and acts
  -- upon it. }

    var
       LINE: LINEINFO;
       CMD:  COMMANDINFO;

begin
   GETLINE (INFILE, LINE);
   PARSECONTROLLINE (LINE, CMD);

   case CMD.NAME of
      SINGLESPACE: SETSPACING (SINGLE, PAGE);
```

Blank Lines

```
      DOUBLESPACE: SETSPACING (DOUBLE, PAGE);

      HEADER:      SETHEADER (CMD.STRINGARG, CMD.STRINGLEN);

      NEXTPAGE:    NEWPAGE (OUTFILE, PAGE);

      PARAGRAPH:   MODE := PARAGRAPHSTYLE;

      VERBATIM:    MODE := VERBATIMSTYLE;

      CENTER:      MODE := CENTERED;

      INDENT:      INDENTATION := CMD.NUMERICARG;

      NOSPLIT:     SETNOSPLIT (CMD.NUMERICARG, OUTFILE, PAGE);

      ERROR:       PRINTERRORLINE (LINE, OUTFILE, PAGE)
   end
end;
```

Blank Lines

This is a good example of the use of strategic blank lines. If the blank lines are removed within the case statement, the result is a much less readable piece of text, with traces of the "blur" of code. Note also the alignment of the alternatives in the case statement. This is quite appropriate. A case statement is a kind of mapping for input values to access.

Pascal

```
begin { -- Main program }
   RESET (INFILE);
   REWRITE (OUTFILE);

   INDENTATION := 0;
   MODE := PARAGRAPHSTYLE;
   STARTDOCUMENT (OUTFILE, PAGE);

   while MOREDATA(INFILE) do begin
```

Design

```
      if NEXTCHAR(INFILE) = CONTROLCHAR then
         DOCOMMANDLINE ({updating} MODE, INDENTATION,
                                    INFILE, OUTFILE, PAGE)

      else if MODE = PARAGRAPHSTYLE then
         FORMATPARAGRAPHS ({using}    INDENTATION,
                            {updating} INFILE, OUTFILE, PAGE)

      else if MODE = VERBATIMSTYLE then
         COPYVERBATIM ({using}    INDENTATION,
                       {updating} INFILE, OUTFILE, PAGE)

      else { -- MODE = CENTERED }
         CENTERLINES ({using} INDENTATION,
                      {updating} INFILE, OUTFILE, PAGE)
   end;

   FINISHDOCUMENT (OUTFILE, PAGE)
end.
```

Pascal

One of the annoying features of Pascal is that the main program is listed last. Ideally the main program should be listed just after the constant, type, and variable declarations given after the program header. This uncomfortable situation means that we always have to refer to definitions that are pages away from the main program in order to interpret the main program.

Design

The body of the main program captures the major design decisions for this program. Its clarity is manifest by the simple and clear while loop that governs the operation of the program. Although often a simple main program belies a complicated understructure, this is not the case here.

[Ada, 1983]
Reference Manual for the Ada Programming Language
U.S. Department of Defense, ANSI/MIL-STD-1815A, 1983

[Ada Rationale, 1979]
Rationale for the Design of the Green Programming Language
Honeywell, Inc. and Cii Honeywell Bull
March 1979

[Brooks, 1975]
Frederick P. Brooks
The Mythical Man-Month
Addison-Wesley, Reading, Mass., 1975

[Cave and Maymon, 1984]
William C. Cave and Gilbert W. Maymon
Software Lifecycle Management
Macmillan Publishing Co., New York, 1984

[Clarke et al., 1980]
Lori Clarke, Jack Wileden, and Alexander Wolf
"Nesting in Ada Is for the Birds"
Sigplan Notices, Vol. 15, No. 11, November 1980

[Conway et al., 1976]
Richard Conway, David Gries, and E. Zimmerman
A Primer on Pascal
Winthrop Publishers, Cambridge, Mass., 1976

[Curtis, 1981]
Bill Curtis, Editor
Human Factors in Software Development
IEEE Computer Society, Box 80452
Los Angeles, Calif. 90080

[Dahl et al., 1972]
O. J. Dahl, C. A. R. Hoare, and E. W. Dijkstra
Structured Programming
Academic Press, New York, 1972

[Dunsmore and Gannon, 1979]
H. E. Dunsmore and John Gannon
"Data Referencing: An Empirical Investigation"
Computer, December 1979

[Fairley, 1985]
Richard Fairley
Software Engineering Concepts
McGraw-Hill, New York, 1985

[Good et al., 1984]
Michael Good, John Whiteside, Dennis Wixon, and Sandy Jones
"Building a User-Derived Interface"
Communications of the ACM, October 1984

[Gries, 1981]
David Gries
The Science of Programming
Springer-Verlag, New York, 1981

[Hoare, 1981]
C.A.R. Hoare
"The Emperor's Old Clothes"
Communications of the ACM, February 1981

[Jensen and Wirth, 1974]
Kathleen Jensen and Niklaus Wirth
Pascal User Manual and Report, Third Edition
Springer-Verlag, New York, 1985

[Ledgard et al., 1979]
Henry Ledgard, Jon Hueras, and Paul Nagin
Pascal With Style
Hayden Book Company, Rochelle Park, N.J., 1979

[Ledgard and Marcotty, 1975]
Henry Ledgard and Michael Marcotty
"A Genealogy of Control Structures"
Communications of the ACM, November 1975

[Levy, 1985]
Leon S. Levy
Software Economics (in preparation)
AT&T Bell Labs, Whippany, N.J., 1985

[Levy, 1985]
Leon S. Levy
"Metaprogramming Method and Its Economic Justification"
(informal manuscript) AT&T Bell Labs, Whippany, N.J., 1985

[Macro and Buxton, 1986]
Allen Macro and John Buxton
The Craft of Software Engineering
(in preparation) Addison-Wesley, Wokingham, Berks, England

[Marcotty and Ledgard, 1986]
Michael Marcotty and Henry Ledgard
The Programming Language Landscape, Second Edition
SRA, Chicago, 1986

[Myers, 1978]
Glenford Myers
Composite/Structured Design
Van Nostrand Reinhold, New York, 1978

[Rubenstein and Hersh, 1984]
Richard Rubenstein and Harry Hersh
The Human Factor
Digital Press, Burlington Mass., 1984

[Singer et al., 1980]
Andrew Singer, Henry Ledgard, and Jon Hueras
"The Annotated Assistant: A step towards human engineering"
IEEE Transactions on Software Engineering, Vol. SE-7, No. 4, 1980

[Sommerville, 1985]
Ian Sommerville
Software Engineering, Second Edition
Addison-Wesley, Reading, Mass., 1985

[Standard Pascal]
The American Pascal Standard, with Annotations
Annotated by Henry Ledgard
Springer-Verlag, New York, 1984

[Standard Pascal]
American National Standard Pascal Computer Programming Language
ANSI-IEEE 770 X3.97-1983

[Weinberg, 1971]
Gerald M. Weinberg
The Psychology of Computer Programming
Van Nostrand Reinhold, New York, 1971

[Wirth, 1971]
Niklaus Wirth
"The Programmng Language Pascal"
Acta Informatica Vol. 1, No. 1, 1971

[Wirth, 1983]
Niklaus Wirth
Programming in Modula-2, Second corrected edition
Springer-Verlag, New York, 1983

[Wulf and Shaw, 1973]
William Wulf and Mary Shaw
"Global Variables Considered Harmful"
Sigplan Notices, August 1973

[Yourdon, 1979]
Edward Yourdon
Managing the Structured Techniques
Prentice-Hall, Englewood Cliffs N.J., 1979

Index

A

Ada®   *Preface*, 146
Abbreviation   6, 30-32, 36
Accuracy   27, 35
Algol 68   112
Alignment   77
Annotation   40-42
Array   58, 60, 147, 161
    packed   147
Assignment operator   66
Asterisks   49
At sign   153-156
Authors   183

B

Balance   3
Basic   10, 38
Black box   104, 112
Blank lines   4, 69, 74, 77, 201, 217
Blank space   77
Boolean   28, 29, 96, 106
    flags   106
    value   28,29
    variables   106
Break character   150-153
Brevity   35
Buxton, John   *Preface*

C

Case statements   72, 146-148
Cave, William   *Preface*
Checkerboard   25
Coarse golfer   118
Code restructuring   45
Comb structures   69-74, 75
Comments   38-51, 69, 142, 183, 189
    avoiding   45
    dribbling   46
    format   47-50

    header   50, 207, 211
    inline   50, 221

    introductory   45, 47
    marker   43-44, 50
    parameter   197
    with content   44-47
Compilation
    separate   113
Compression   4
Conceptual units   67
Conditional statements   86
Constant declaration   4
Constants   36, 191
    magic   33
Context   29, 30, 36
Control structures   84-88, 146, 161
    one-in, one-out   84-86, 161-163
Conway, Richard   120
Correctness   120-124
    adversary   121
    compiler   120
    programmer   120
    runtime   120
    specification   121
    user   121
Craftsmanship   2, 180

D

Date   183
Declaration   34, 95
    constant   4
    global   113
    header   115
    type   130
Documentation   17, 18, 45
    external   45
    self   183

Dunsmore, H. E.   100

E

Error   56, 189
    counting   122